NYC GIFTED & TALENTED TEST PREP

Pre-K and Kindergarten

NNAT®2/3 WORKBOOK
OLSAT®-8 WORKBOOK

FOR AGES 4-6

Written by
Origins
Publications

Copyright © Origins Publications

IBSN: 978-1-948255-51-6

COLOR EDITION

All rights reserved. This book or any portion thereof may not be reproduced or used in any manner whatsoever without the express written permission of the publisher.

The Naglieri Nonverbal Ability Test® (NNAT®2/3) is a registered trademark of NCS Pearson Inc., which is not affiliated with Origins Publications.

The Otis-Lennon School Ability Test (OLSAT®) is a registered trademark of NCS Pearson, which is not affiliated with Origins Publications. NCS Pearson has not endorsed the contents of this book.

Table of Contents

About Origins Tutoring 3

NYC G&T Test Overview and Test Prep Tips 4

A. NNAT-2 Workbook

NNAT-2 Skill-Building Exercises 9

    What Does Not Belong 10

    Connecting and Taking Apart Shapes 14

    Puzzles and Patterns 21

    Sequences 28

NNAT-2 Practice Questions 32

    Pattern Completion 33

    Reasoning by Analogy 52

    Serial Reasoning 63

NNAT-2 Answer Keys 72

B. OLSAT Workbook

OLSAT Practice Questions 74

    Following Directions 75

    Aural Reasoning 85

    Arithmetic Reasoning 93

OLSAT Answer Keys 103

OLSAT Supplemental Activities 104

About Origins Tutoring

We support students in developing the skills to think, learn and problem solve on their own. Students who work with us commit to success because we inspire them to invest in their own future.

Our expertise is in helping preschool and elementary students develop their higher-order thinking skills while also improving their chances of admission into gifted and accelerated-learner programs in NYC.

Please contact us with any questions you have about the NYC Gifted and Talented school process.

We are here to help you!

info@originstutoring.com
www.originstutoring.com

BONUS NNAT® and OLSAT® PRACTICE TESTS

Don't forget to download our bonus practice tests to help your child prepare for the actual test.

The bonus practice tests are available on our website.

Please visit **www.originstutoring.com/bonus-test-7** to access the NNAT® bonus test.

Please visit **www.originstutoring.com/bonus-test-14** to access the OLSAT® bonus test.

These bonus tests will help your child get used to the different materials presented on the official tests and become more familiarized with the process of taking a standardized test.

The NYC Gifted and Talented (G&T) Test

Overview

The NYC Gifted and Talented test is designed to assess the cognitive skills that relate to academic success in school for students between four and seven. Children take the test to try to gain admissions into NYC gifted and talented schools and programs.

The questions on the NYC Gifted and Talented test are pulled from two widely used gifted assessments: the Naglieri Nonverbal Ability Test – the NNAT®2/3, and the Otis-Lennon School Ability Test - OLSAT®.

Content and Format

The NNAT® portion of the test consists of geometric figures, shapes, and symbols. A child must use visual reasoning and spatial thinking skills to decipher the answers.

Since the NNAT® requires very little language spoken, it is considered a good indicator of raw intelligence as it does not discriminate against children whose are unable to read, write or speak in the English Language.

The OLSAT® portion of the test consists of questions that measure a student's ability to gather and manipulate information from language. To answer these questions, a student needs to be able to fully understand what a question is asking, and make inferences based on what she has heard. A student also benefits from a broad vocabulary knowledge.

Note that although the official OLSAT® has a **nonverbal and verbal section**, the NYC Gifted and Talented test only includes **OLSAT® verbal questions.**

Although a child needs to understand some verbal language for the OLSAT® sections, all answer choices are shown in a picture format for the NYC Gifted and Talented test.

The **NNAT®** portion of the test has **48 multiple-choice questions.**

The **OLSAT®** portion of the test has **30 multiple-choice questions.**

New York City teachers, trained in giving both assessments, administer the test to your child. The teacher will take your child to a separate room. After reading some general instructions and going through a few sample questions - so your child can know what to expect - they will give the test to your child.

The administrator will give your child frequent breaks in between sets of questions. The administrator will read the questions to your child for the OLSAT® test, but one time only. The one-time reading of the question is strictly enforced because the exam is measuring how well your child comprehends and retains information, and reading the question once is one way in which the test assesses this skill.

You can pick the language you want your child to take the test in. Options are: Arabic, Bengali, Chinese (Cantonese and Mandarin), French, Haitian Creole, Korean, Russian, Spanish and Urdu. Your child cannot change back and forth between languages during the test.

Scoring

Though the NNAT® (nonverbal) section includes more questions, it does not count more than the OLSAT® (verbal) section. Each section is weighted equally, accounting for half of a child's score.

The OLSAT® and NNAT® sections are graded separately, and the raw scores (the total number of questions answered correctly) are then converted to individual percentile ranks for each test. These are then combined to form a composite score, or, overall percentile score. This overall score is what the gifted and talented programs will look at when assessing your child.

Exam Length

The exam is untimed, but expect your child to spend between one and two hours at a testing centre.

How to Use this Book

This book will help your child get used to the format and content of the test so she will be adequately prepared and feel confident on test day.

The more your child is familiar with the questions on the NYC Gifted and

Talented test, the better she or he will fare when taking the test.

In this book, you'll find:

A NNAT®2/3 workbook, which includes:

- 84 skill-builder exercises to help your child improve the logical and visual reasoning skills required to excel on the test.
- 90 NNAT®2/3 practice questions covering the three NNAT® question types on this test: **Pattern Completion, Reasoning by Analogy, Serial Reasoning**.
- Detailed descriptions of question types.
- Teaching tips to help your child approach each test type strategically and with confidence.

An OLSAT® workbook, which includes:

- 25 **Following Directions** practice questions.
- 20 **Aural Reasoning** practice questions.
- 25 **Arithmetic Reasoning** practice questions.
- Detailed descriptions of question types, including the concepts and skills they assess.
- Teaching tips to help your child approach each question type strategically and with confidence.

We suggest you begin by helping your child go through the NNAT®2 skill-building exercises.

These exercises provide an opportunity for students to learn the concepts and strengthen the fundamental skills required to successfully tackle questions on the official exam.

The skill-building activities are followed by NNAT® and OLSAT® practice questions, divided into sections based on the question types found on the NYC Gifted and Talented test.

Please use the teaching tips provided at the beginning of each of these sections to guide your child as he or she progresses through the questions.

We suggest you try make sure that your student has enough time before the actual test date to go through at least half of all the practice questions.

Please note that the NNAT® questions on the current G&T test have only two colors: blue and yellow. In this book, we use multiple colors to keep your child interested as he or she progresses through the many skill-builder exercises and practice questions. The BONUS tests you can download from our website are in the official colors of the NNAT®2. Get the link on page 3 of this book.

On the official G&T test, the OLSAT® consists of black and white graphic images, which resemble the images in the practice questions presented in this book and the downloadable test (see page 3).

Test Prep Tips and Strategies

Firstly, and most importantly, commit to making the test preparation process a stress-free one. Helping your child keep calm and focused in the face of challenge is a quality that will benefit him throughout his academic life.

Be prepared for difficult questions from the get-go! There will be a certain percentage of questions that are very challenging for all kids. It is key to encourage your child to use all strategies available to him or her when faced with challenging questions. And remember that your kid can get quite a few questions wrong and still do very well on the test.

Before starting a section, read the teaching tips provided at the beginning. They will help you guide your student as he or she progresses through the practice questions in that section.

These additional strategies may also be useful as you help your child prepare:

Before You Start
- Find a quiet, comfortable spot to work free of distractions.
- Tell your child you will be doing some fun activities together.
- Show your child how to perform the simple technique of shading (and erasing) bubbles. If your child is in pre-K, she will only have to point at the correct answer.

During Prep

- If your child is challenged by a question, ask your child to explain why he or she chose a specific answer. If the answer was incorrect, this will help you identify where your child is stumbling. If the answer was correct, asking your child to articulate her reasoning aloud will help reinforce the concept.

- Encourage your child to carefully **consider all the answer options** before selecting one. Tell her there is only ONE answer.

- If your child is stumped by a question, she or he can use the **process of elimination**. First, encourage your child to eliminate obviously wrong answers to narrow down the answer choices. If your child is still in doubt after using this technique, tell him or her to guess as there are no points deducted for wrong answers.

- Review all the questions your student answered incorrectly, and explain to your student why the answer is incorrect. Have your student attempt these questions again a few days later to see if he now understands the concept.

- Encourage your student to do her best, but take plenty of study breaks. Start with 10-15 minute sessions. Your student will perform best if she views these activities as fun and engaging, not as exercises to be avoided.

- NNAT® tip: Encourage your child to visualize the correct answer in the empty box before checking the answer options.

- OLSAT® tip: Before each question, tell your student that she or he needs to listen carefully and pay full attention to the question.

- OLSAT® tip: Encourage your student to look at the answer options while you read the questions.

When To Start Preparing

Every family and student will approach preparation for this test differently. There is no 'right' way to prepare; there is only the best way for a particular child and family.

We suggest students, at minimum, take one full-length practice test and spend 8-12 hours working through practice questions.

If you have limited time to prepare, spend most energy reviewing areas where your child is encountering the majority of problems.

As they say, knowledge is power! Preparing for the G&T test will certainly help your child avoid anxiety and make sure she does not give up too soon when faced with unfamiliar and perplexing questions.

NNAT® 2/3
Skill-building Exercises

The skill-building exercises are divided into five sections:

What Does Not Belong

Connecting and Taking Apart Shapes

Patterns and Puzzles

Sequences

These exercises were designed to help your child learn the concepts and strengthen the fundamental skills required to successfully tackle questions on the official NNAT®2/3 test.

The activities will help develop your child's ability to identify:

- differences in visual figures and shapes;
- how shapes and figures appear when combined or separated;
- how a shape and/or figure transforms by sliding, flipping, or rotating;
- when a shape or figure repeats to complete a pattern; and
- how shapes and figures progress sequentially according to a rule.

What Does Not Belong

This skill-building section helps your child develop his or her ability to identify differences in visual figures and shapes.

In the "What Does Not Belong" exercises, ask your child to identify which of the five pictures does not belong with the others in the row.

Example:

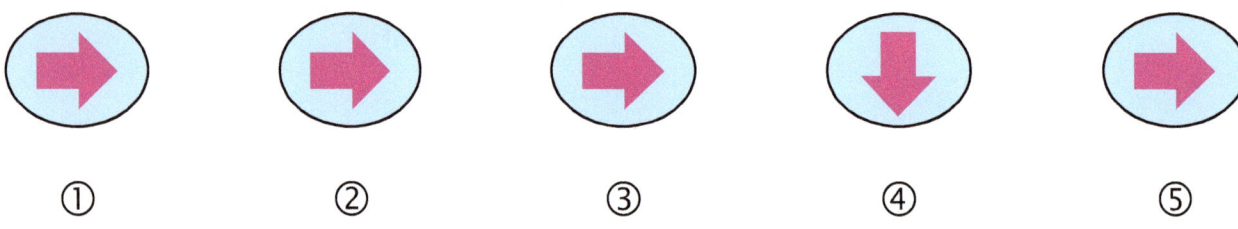

① ② ③ ④ ⑤

Explanation: In the row above, there are five pictures. The one that does not belong with the others is option choice 4. In this picture, the pink arrow inside the blue circle is pointing downwards. In the other pictures, the pink arrow is pointing to the side.

Which shape does not belong with others?

1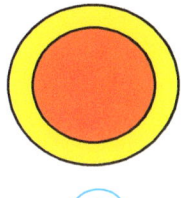

2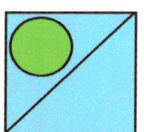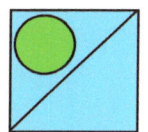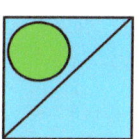

3

4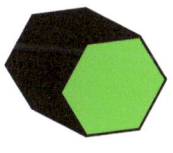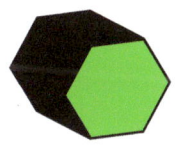

5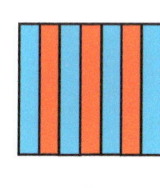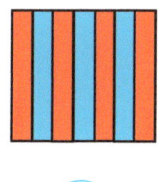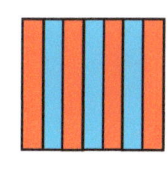

Which shape does not belong with others?

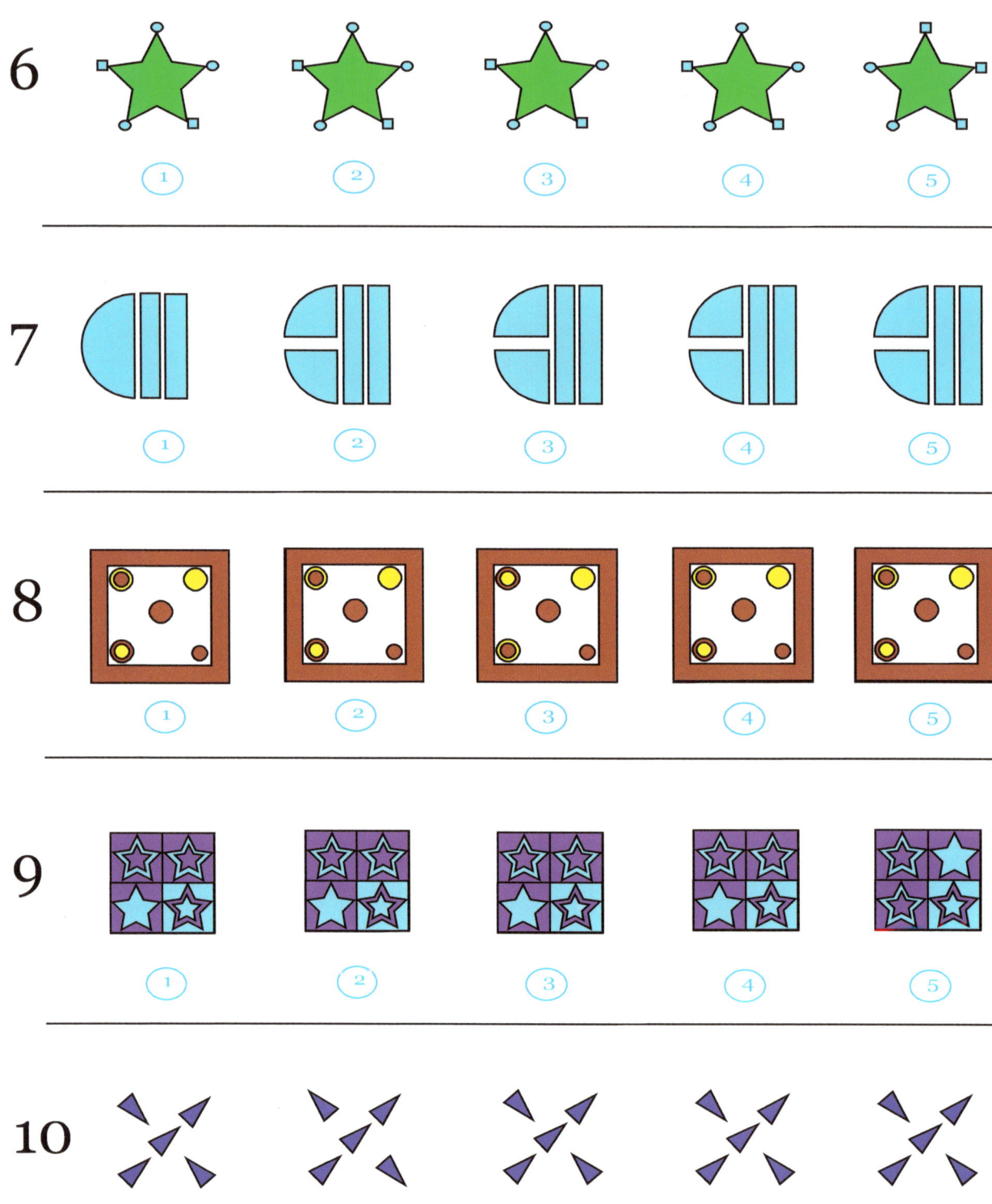

Which shape does not belong with others?

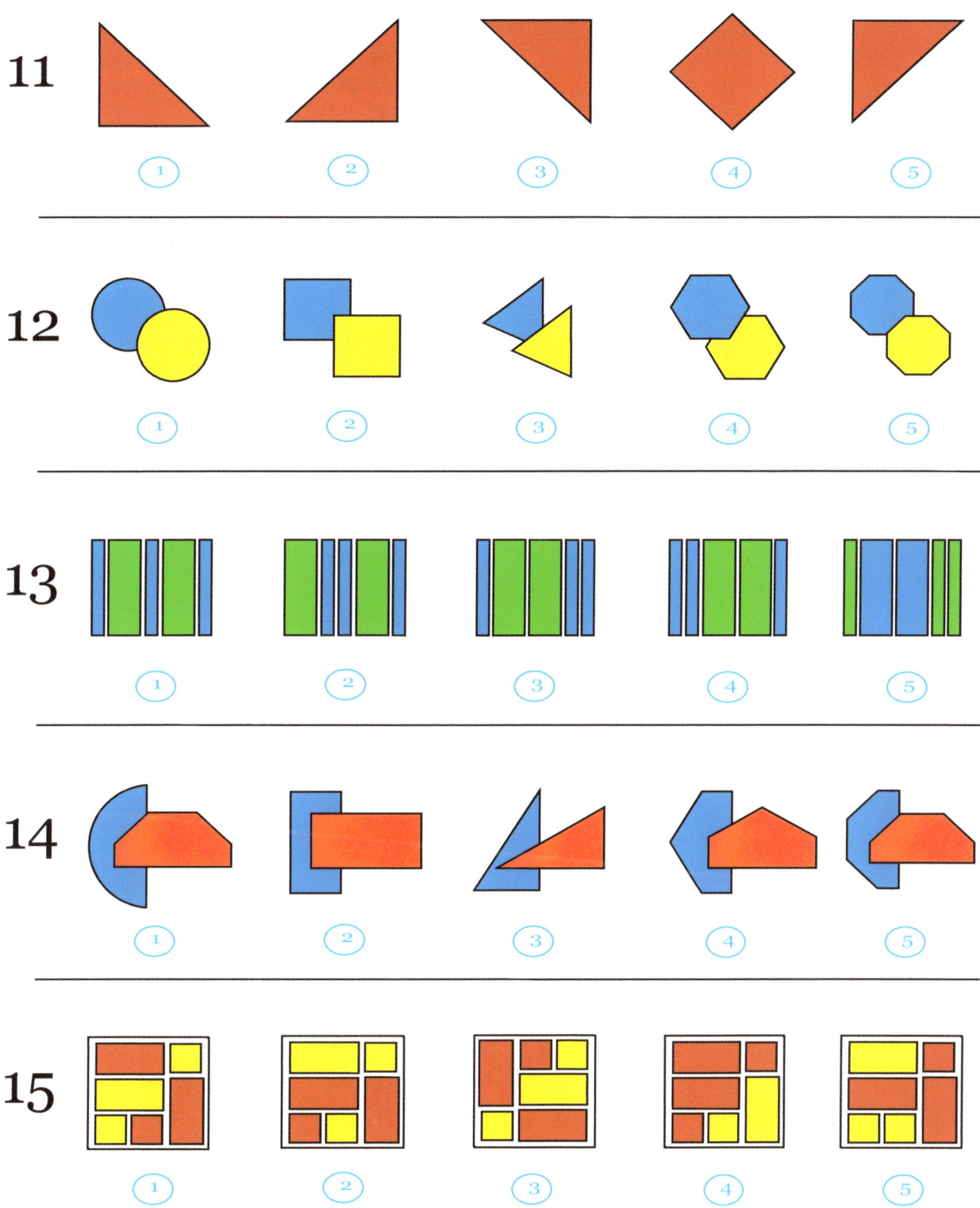

Connecting & Taking Apart Shapes

This skill-building section helps your child develop his or her ability to identify differences in visual figures and shapes, and how shapes and figures appear when combined or separated.

In the first exercises (**Connecting Shapes**), ask your child to identify what the two shapes at the beginning of the row would look like when they are connected together.

Example:

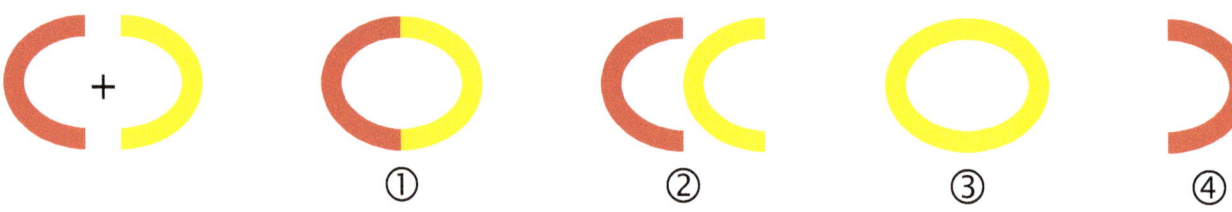

Explanation: At the beginning of row above, there are two curved shapes, one yellow and one red. When these two shapes are connected, they create the shape in option one, which is the correct answer.

In the second exercises (**Taking Apart Shapes**), ask your child to look at the shape at the beginning of the row and identify the two shapes it would become if taken apart. In this exercise, your child must choose two answers.

Example:

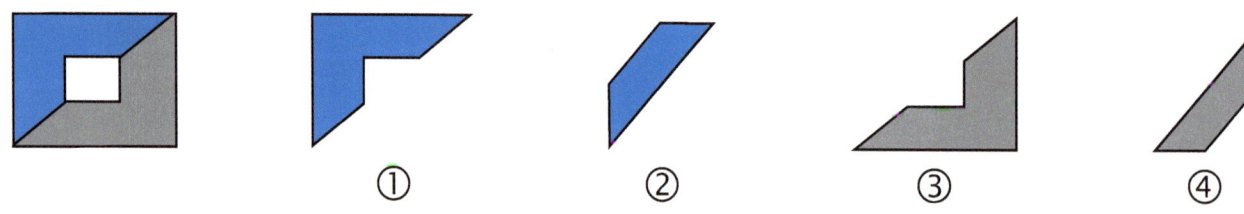

Explanation: At the beginning of row above is a shape with a blue piece and a grey piece. When taken apart, this shape becomes the blue figure in option one and the grey figure in option three, which are the correct answers.

Which shape is created when the first two shapes are connected together?

1   +   = 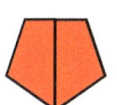

2   +   = 

3      +      = 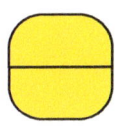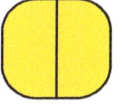

4      +      = 

5      +   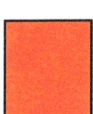   = 

Which shape is created when the first two shapes are connected together?

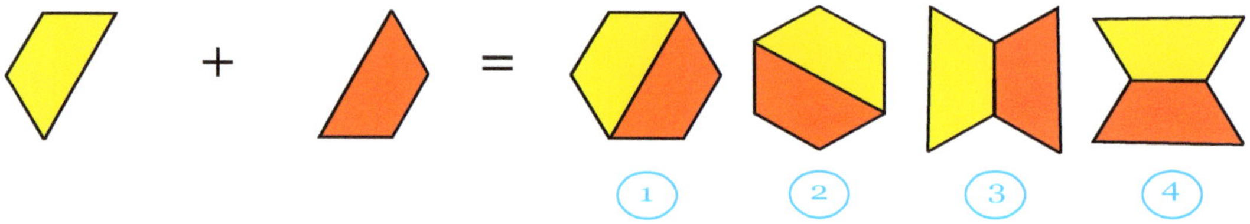

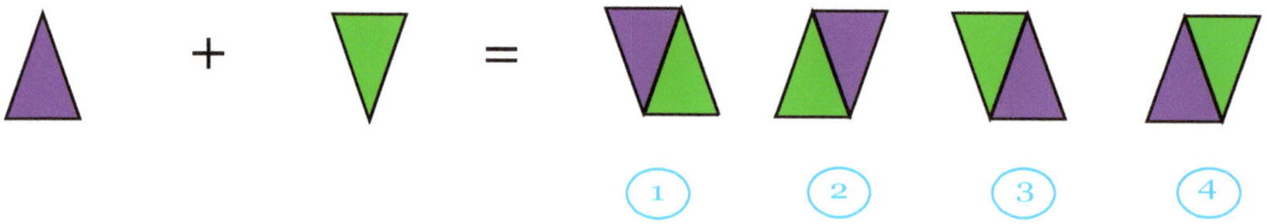

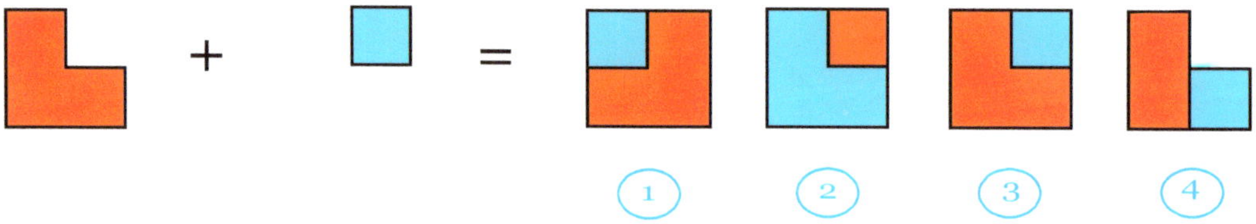

6

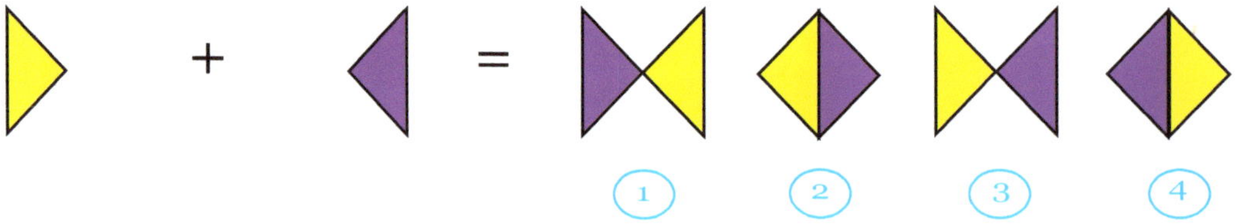

Which shape is created when the first two shapes are connected together?

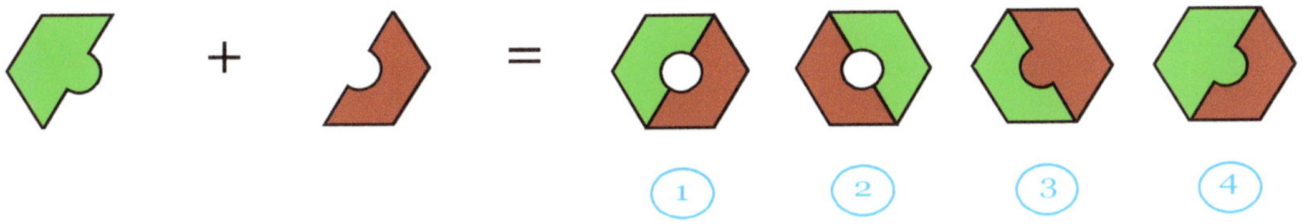

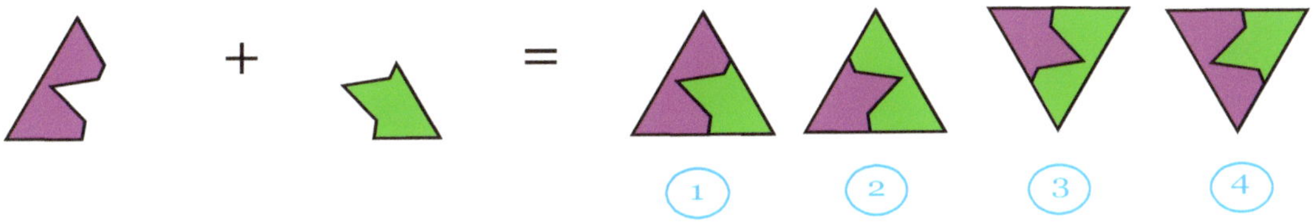

11

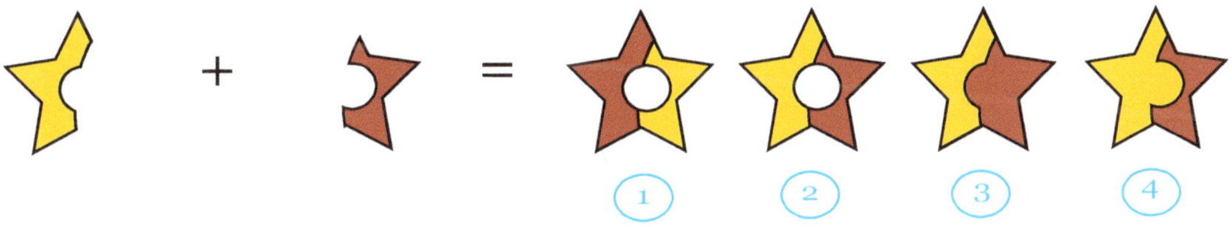

NNAT Skill-Builders

Which two shapes are created when the first shape is taken apart?

1  =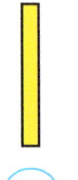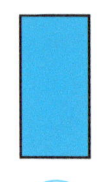
① ② ③ ④

2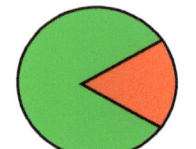
① ② ③ ④

3  =
① ② ③ ④

4
① ② ③ ④

5
① ② ③ ④

Which two shapes are created when the first shape is taken apart?

6  =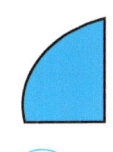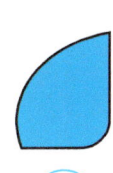

7  =

8 =

9  =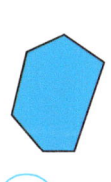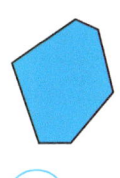

10  =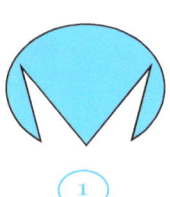

NNAT Skill-Builders

Which two shapes are created when the first shape is taken apart?

11  =  ①  ②  ③  ④

12  =  ① ②  ③  ④

13  =  ① 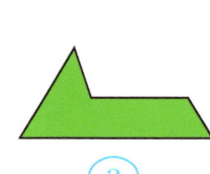 ② 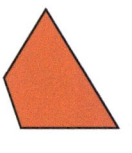 ③ 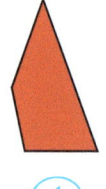 ④

14  =  ① 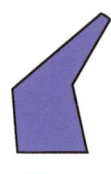 ②  ③ 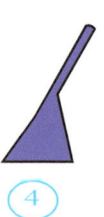 ④

15  =  ①  ② ③  ④

Puzzles and Patterns

These skill-builder activities help your child develop the skills needed to successfully tackle the pattern completion section on the NNAT2.

In the first exercises (**Finding Puzzle Piece**), ask your child to identify, among the answer options, the missing puzzle piece that exactly completes the missing piece of the patterned square at the beginning of the row.

Example:

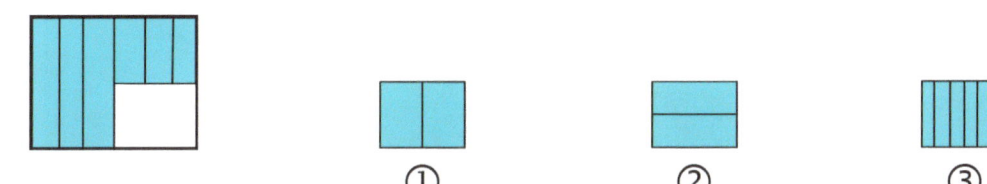

Explanation: At the beginning of the row above is a blue square with vertical black stripes. The picture among the answer options that completes the pattern is option 4, as this 'puzzle piece' would match the stripes exactly if placed into the empty square.

In the second exercises (**Matching Patterns**), ask your child to identify which of the patterns in the answer options matches exactly the pattern presented at the beginning of the row.

Example:

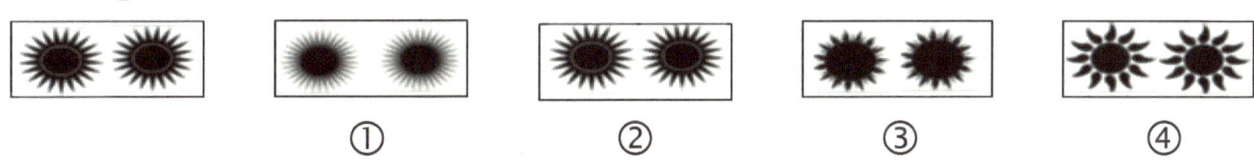

Explanation: At the beginning of row above is a rectangle with black suns. The pattern that matches this initial pattern exactly is shown in answer option 2.

Which piece fits in the white square to complete the puzzle?

1  =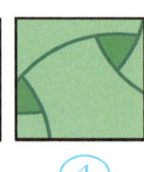

2  =

3  =

4  =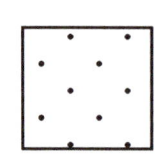

5  =

NNAT Skill-Builders

Which piece fits in the white square to complete the puzzle?

6  =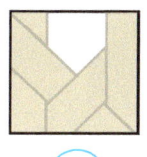
   ① ② ③ ④

7  =
   ① ② ③ ④

8 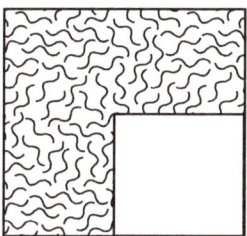 =
   ① ② ③ ④

9  =
   ① ② ③ ④

10  =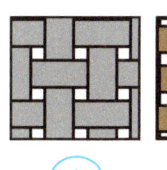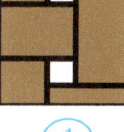
    ① ② ③ ④

NNAT Skill-Builders

Which piece fits in the white square to complete the puzzle?

11 = ① ② ③ ④

12 = ① ② ③ ④

13 = ① ② ③ ④

14 = ① ② ③ ④

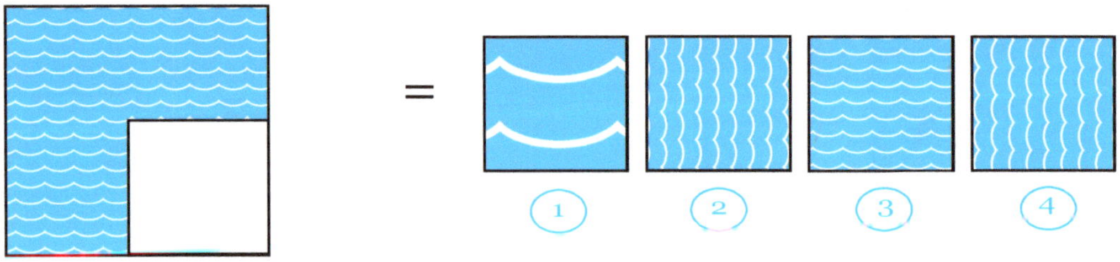

15 = ① ② ③ ④

24

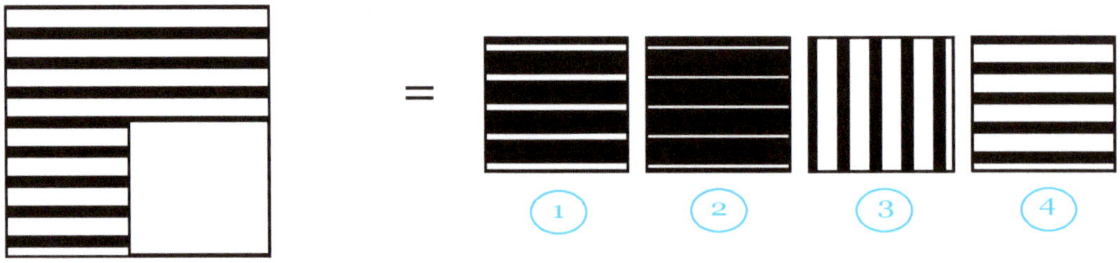

Which pattern matches the pattern at the beginning of the row?

Which pattern matches the pattern at the beginning of the row?

6

7

8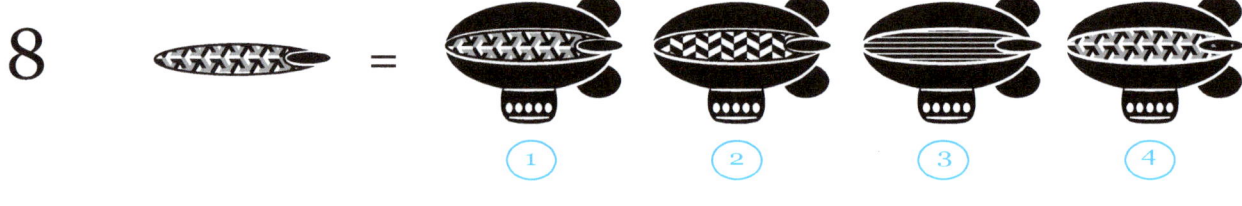

9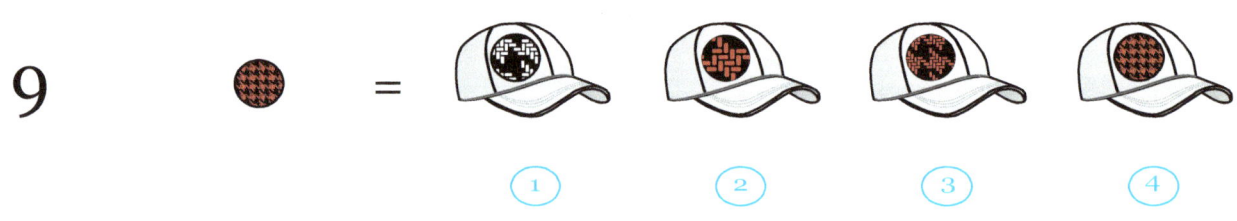

10

Which pattern matches the pattern at the beginning of the row?

11  =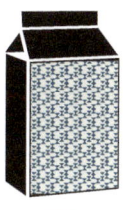

12  =

13 =

14  =

15  =

Sequences

These skill-building activities help your child develop his or her ability to identify how a shape transforms by sliding, flipping, or rotating, and how a shape progresses sequentially according to a rule.

In these exercises, ask your child to look at the first row of pictures and identify which picture in the second row would come next in the sequence (i.e: the picture that would best go in the place represented by the question mark box).

Example:

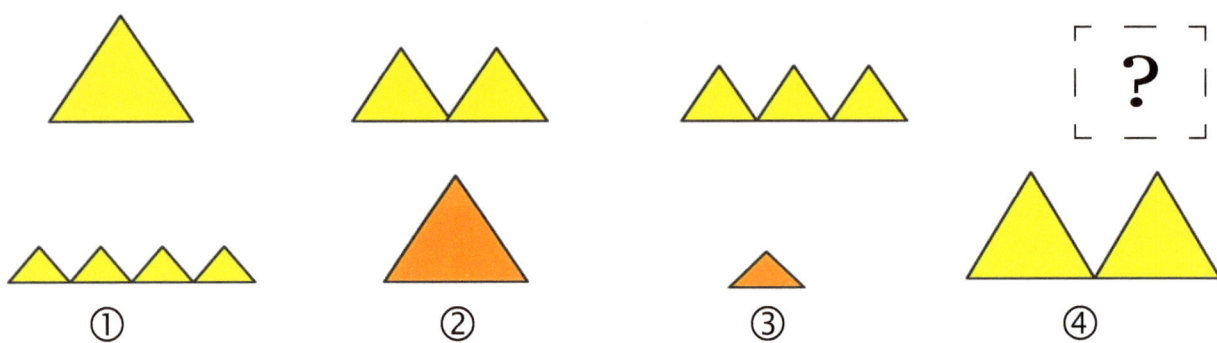

Explanation: In the first row above, the first picture is of one large yellow triangle followed by two smaller yellow triangles in the second picture. The third picture shows three even smaller yellow triangles. The next picture in the series should therefore follows the rule of the sequence which is that each triangle adds an additional one *and* gets smaller as the sequence progresses. Therefore, the correct answer is option 1 (four yellow triangles that are smaller than the three preceding triangles).

Which object in the second row comes next in the sequence?

1

2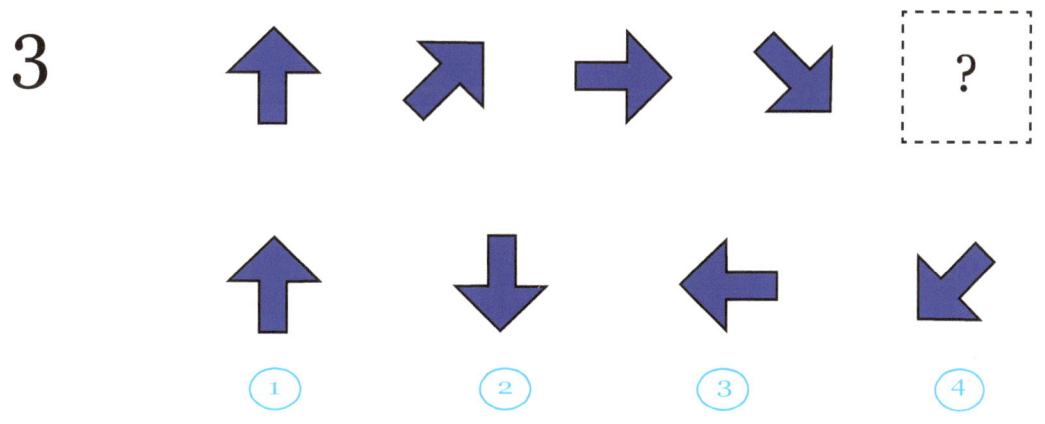

3

Which object in the second row comes next in the sequence?

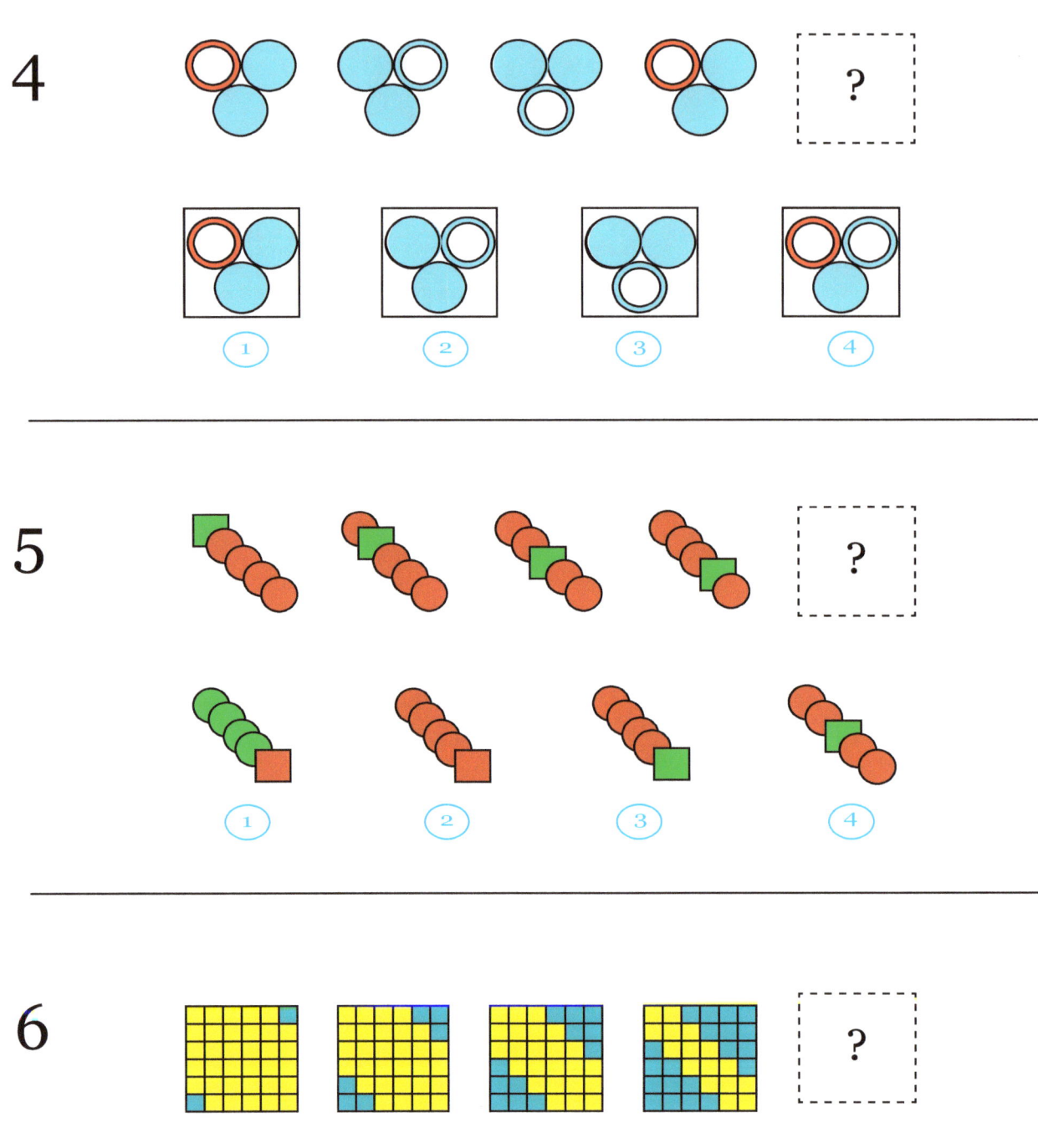

NNAT Skill-Builders

Which object in the second row comes next in the sequence?

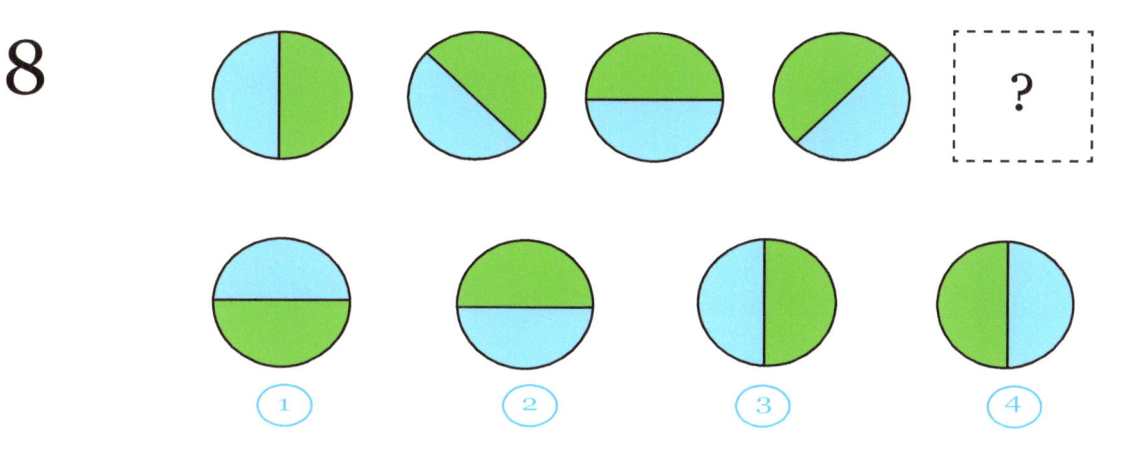

NYC G&T Test Prep Book - Origins Tutoring© Inc. 31

NNAT®2/3 Practice Questions

The NNAT® 2/3 Level A is comprised of three main 'question' types. The following three sections provide practice questions on each of these three question types.

Pattern Completion

Reasoning by Analogy

Serial Reasoning

Each question type involves the following steps:

- The student is presented with a picture of a matrix.
- The student must observe and detect the relationship among the parts of the matrix.
- The student must solve the problem based on the information shown to her within the matrix, and choose the correct answer from five possible options.

Before your child attempts the practice questions, spend a few minutes yourself reviewing the teaching tips for each section so you can be prepared to help your child if he or she struggles with a question.

The NNAT® 2/3 practice questions will help your child use and bolster the skills needed to succeed on the actual test. As you watch your child tackle the practice questions, you will also be able to identify the question types that your child finds most challenging and provide extra practice for him or her in those areas.

Remember to download a bonus NNAT® 2/3 practice test at www.originstutoring.com/bonus-test-7

Pattern Completion

With this question type, the child is presented with a design in a rectangle. Inside the large rectangle is a smaller white rectangle representing a missing piece that completes the design. The child must choose the answer that best fits the inner rectangle so that the missing parts complete the design.

These questions are the most common question types found on the Level A and B tests, and are the easiest kinds of matrices in the exam.

Before each question in this section, say to your child:

"Look at the picture. A piece is missing where you see the question mark. Show me the piece that is missing in the answer choices."

After a few questions, your child will probably not need this prompt and will spontaneously point to or mark an answer.

Tips and Strategies

Ask your student to complete the picture by continuing the correct lines and colors of the design into the empty box. Then, match the drawing with the correct answer choice.

Ask your student to note the shade/color and design next to the corners of the empty box as this is a useful base to help identify the correct answer.

Go through each answer option and ask the student to visualize how each choice would fit the design.

1

2

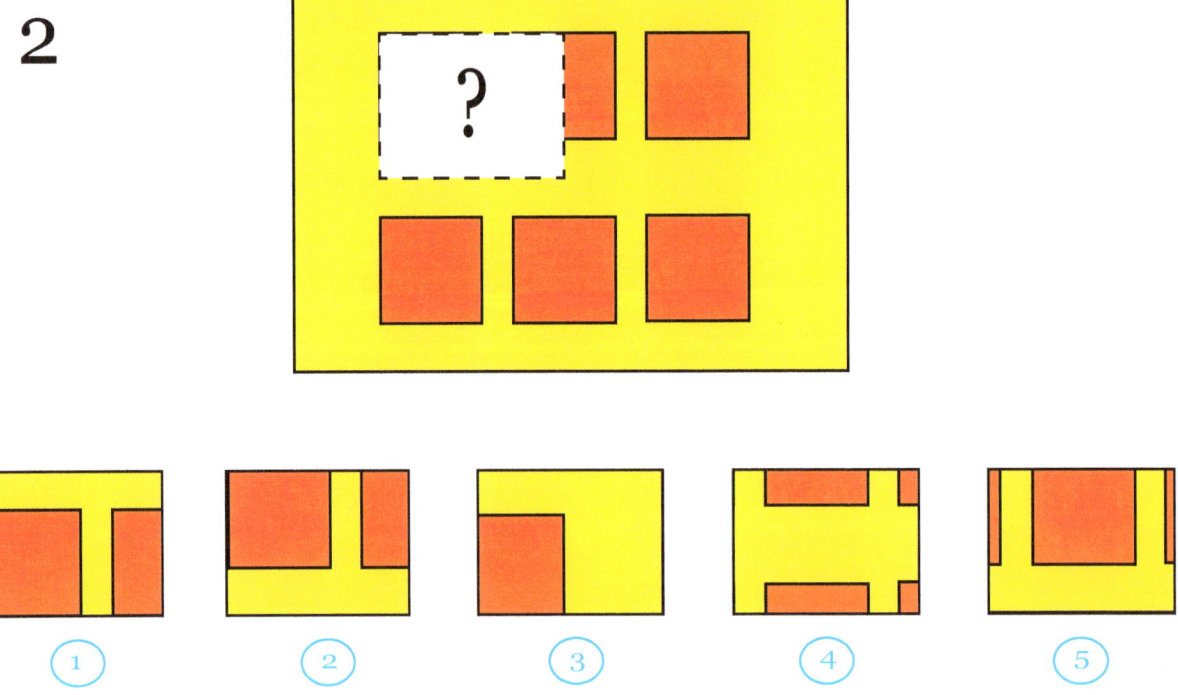

3

    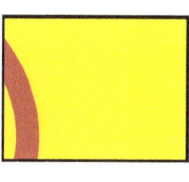

① ② ③ ④ ⑤

4

 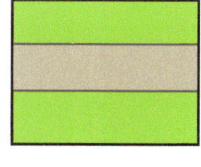  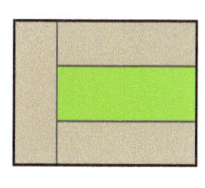 

① ② ③ ④ ⑤

7

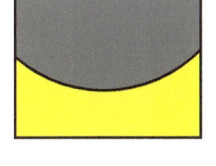 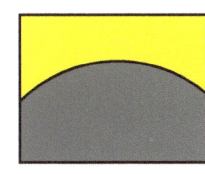 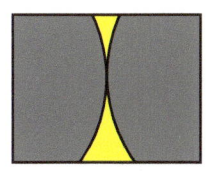 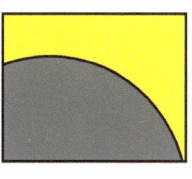 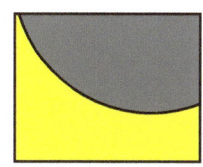

① ② ③ ④ ⑤

8

 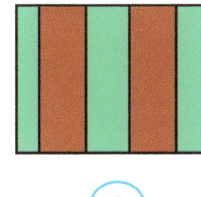 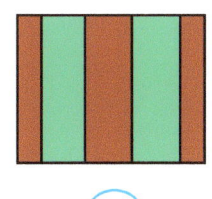  

① ② ③ ④ ⑤

9

10

11

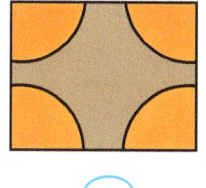  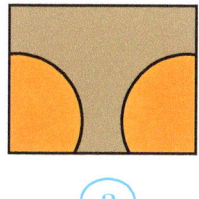 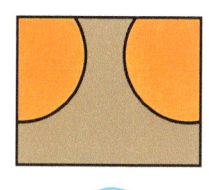 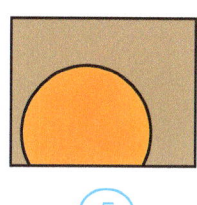

12

 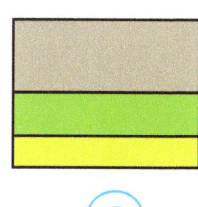  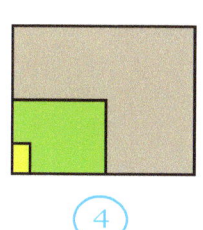 

13

 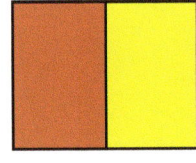   
① ② ③ ④ ⑤

14

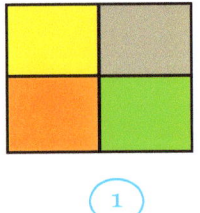    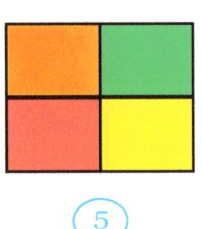
① ② ③ ④ ⑤

15

① ② ③ ④ ⑤

16

   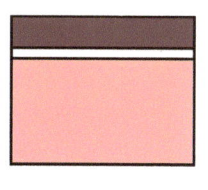 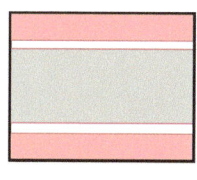
① ② ③ ④ ⑤

17

① ② ③ ④ ⑤

18

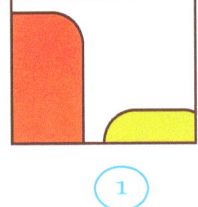 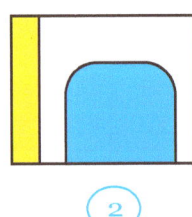 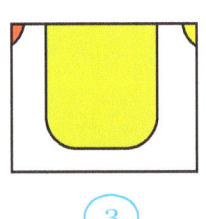 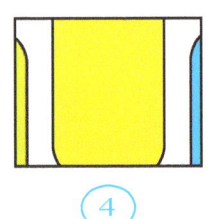 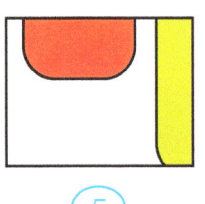
① ② ③ ④ ⑤

19

20

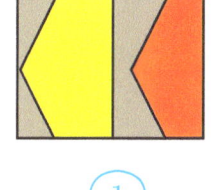  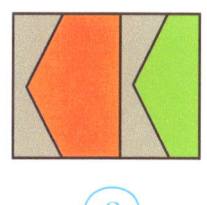 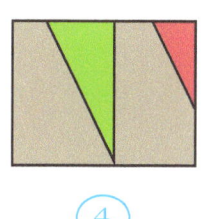 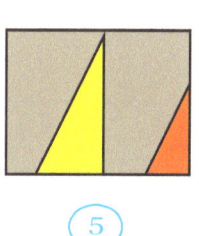

21

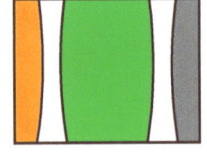 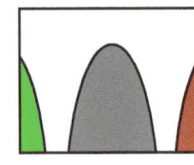 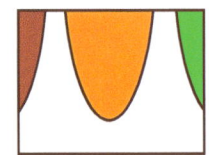 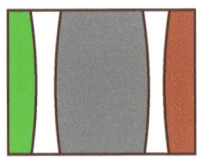 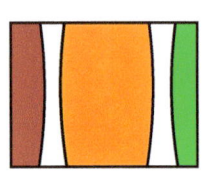
① ② ③ ④ ⑤

22

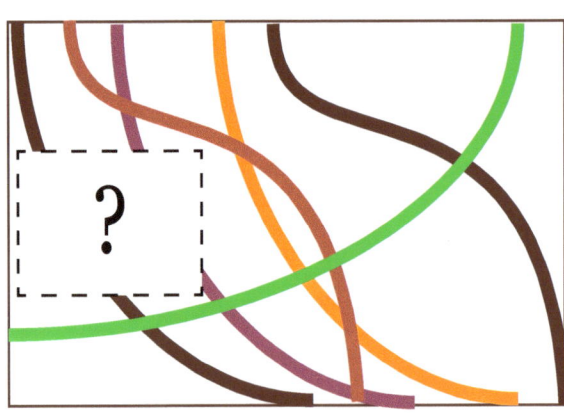

    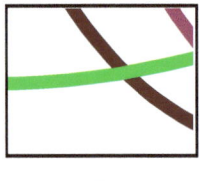
① ② ③ ④ ⑤

23

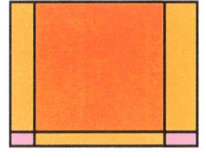 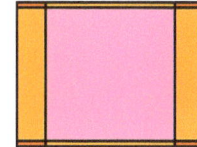   
① ② ③ ④ ⑤

24

   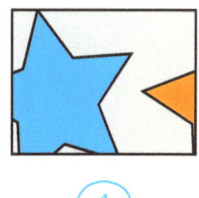 
① ② ③ ④ ⑤

25

   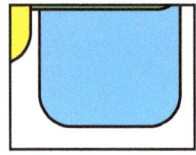   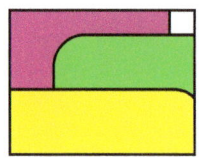   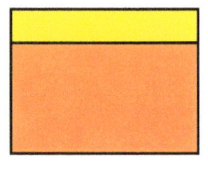   

① ② ③ ④ ⑤

26

      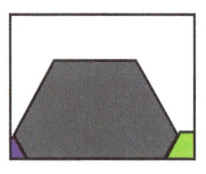   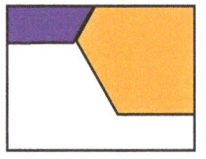   

① ② ③ ④ ⑤

27

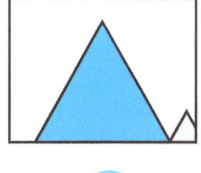    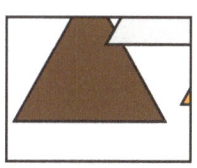
① ② ③ ④ ⑤

28

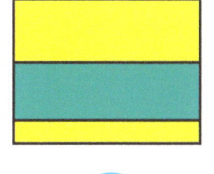 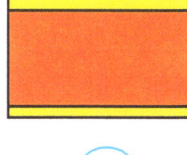 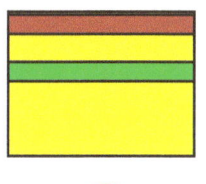  
① ② ③ ④ ⑤

29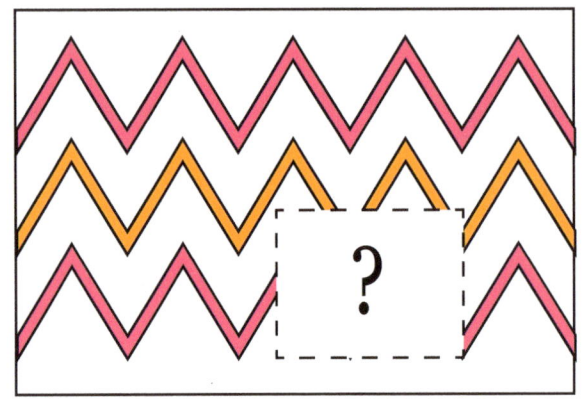

① ② ③ ④ ⑤

30

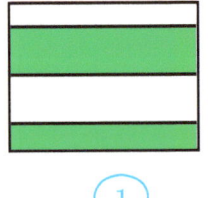    
① ② ③ ④ ⑤

31

Yes

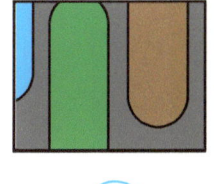  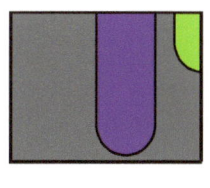 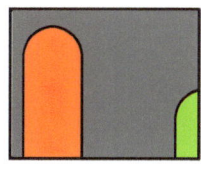 
① ② ③ ④ ⑤

32

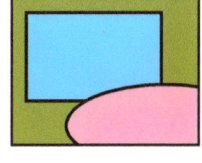    
① ② ③ ④ ⑤

33

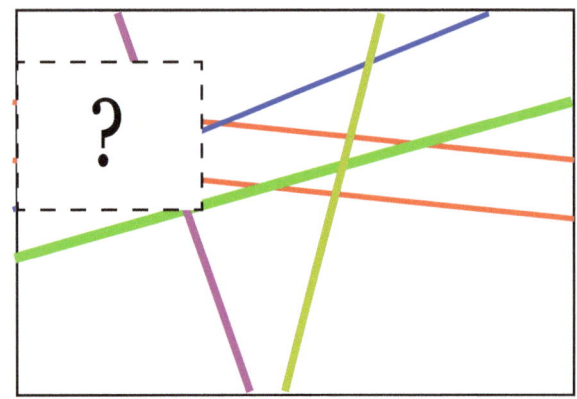

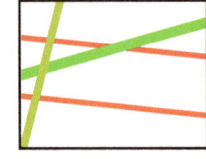         

① ② ③ ④ ⑤

34

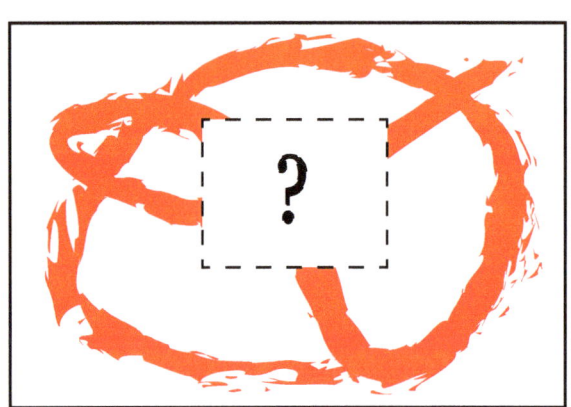

① ② ③ ④ ⑤

35

  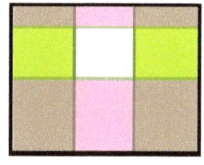 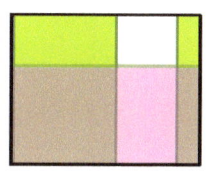 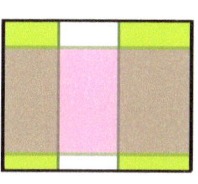
① ② ③ ④ ⑤

36

   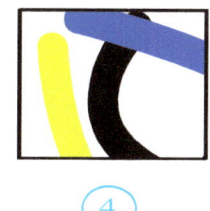 
① ② ③ ④ ⑤

Reasoning by Analogy

With this question type, the child is presented with a matrix of 4-6 boxes containing objects, usually geometric shapes.

To solve the problem, the child must determine how the object changes as it moves across the row and down the column in the matrix. The question may require that the student pay close attention to several aspects of the design (e.g: shading, shape) at the same time.

Before each question in this section, say to your child:

"Look at the picture. A piece is missing where you see the question mark. Show me the piece that is missing in the answer choices."

Tips and Strategies

Make sure your student knows key concepts that come up in these types of questions, including geometric concepts such as rotational symmetry, line symmetry, parts of a whole.

If your student is finding these items difficult, encourage her to discover the pattern by looking in each direction (horizontally and vertically).

- Ask: "How do the objects change in the first row? Do you see a pattern? Do the objects change in the same way in the second row? The third row?"
- Ask: "How do the objects change in the first column? Do you see a pattern? Do the objects change in the same way in the second column? The third column?"

Encourage your student to isolate one element (e.g: outer shape, inner shape/s) and identify how it changes:

- Is the shading of the element changing as it moves?
- Is the element changing positions as it moves? Does it move up or down? Clockwise or counter-clockwise? Does it end up in the opposite (mirror) position?
- Does the element disappear and appear again as it move along the row/column? Does it get bigger or smaller?

Encourage your student to make a prediction for the missing object and compare the description with the answer choices.

1

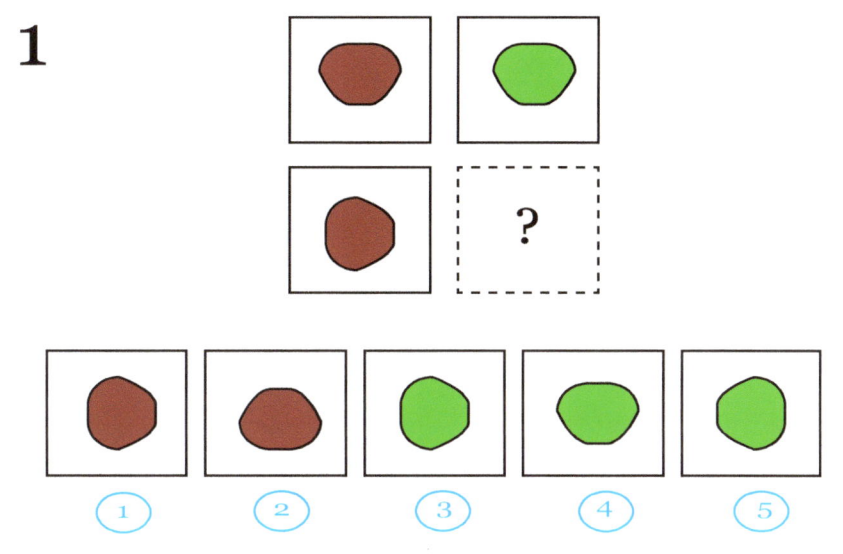

2

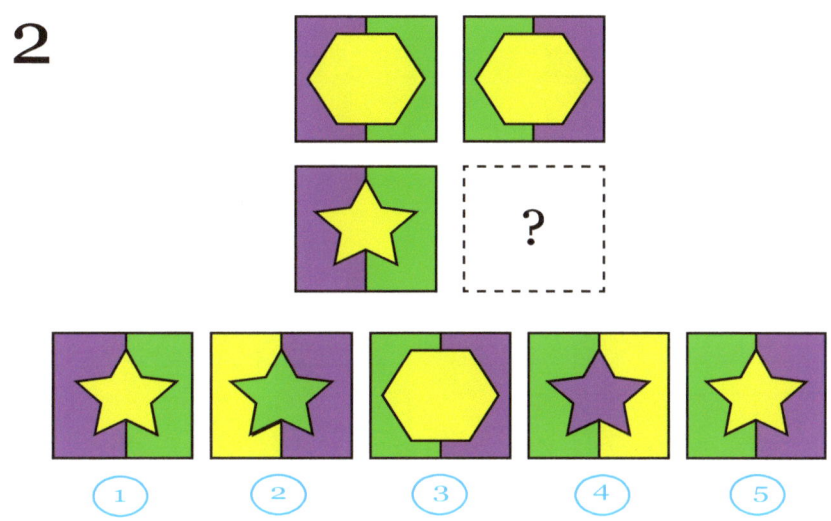

3

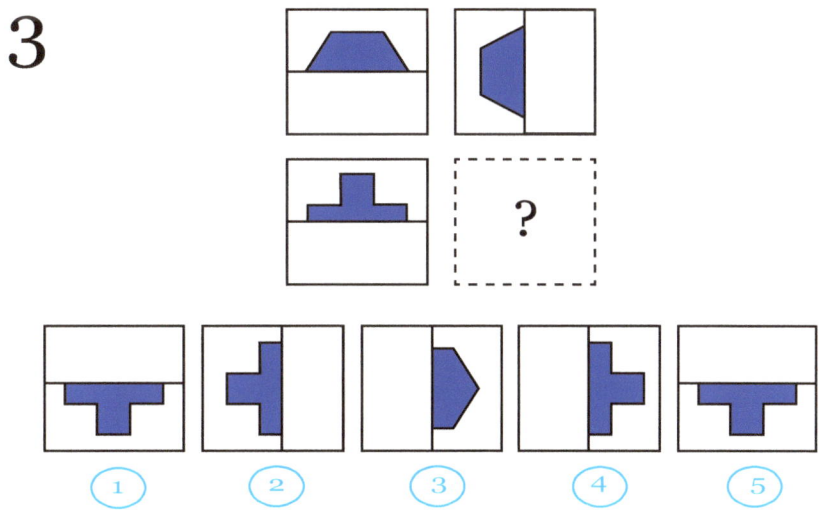

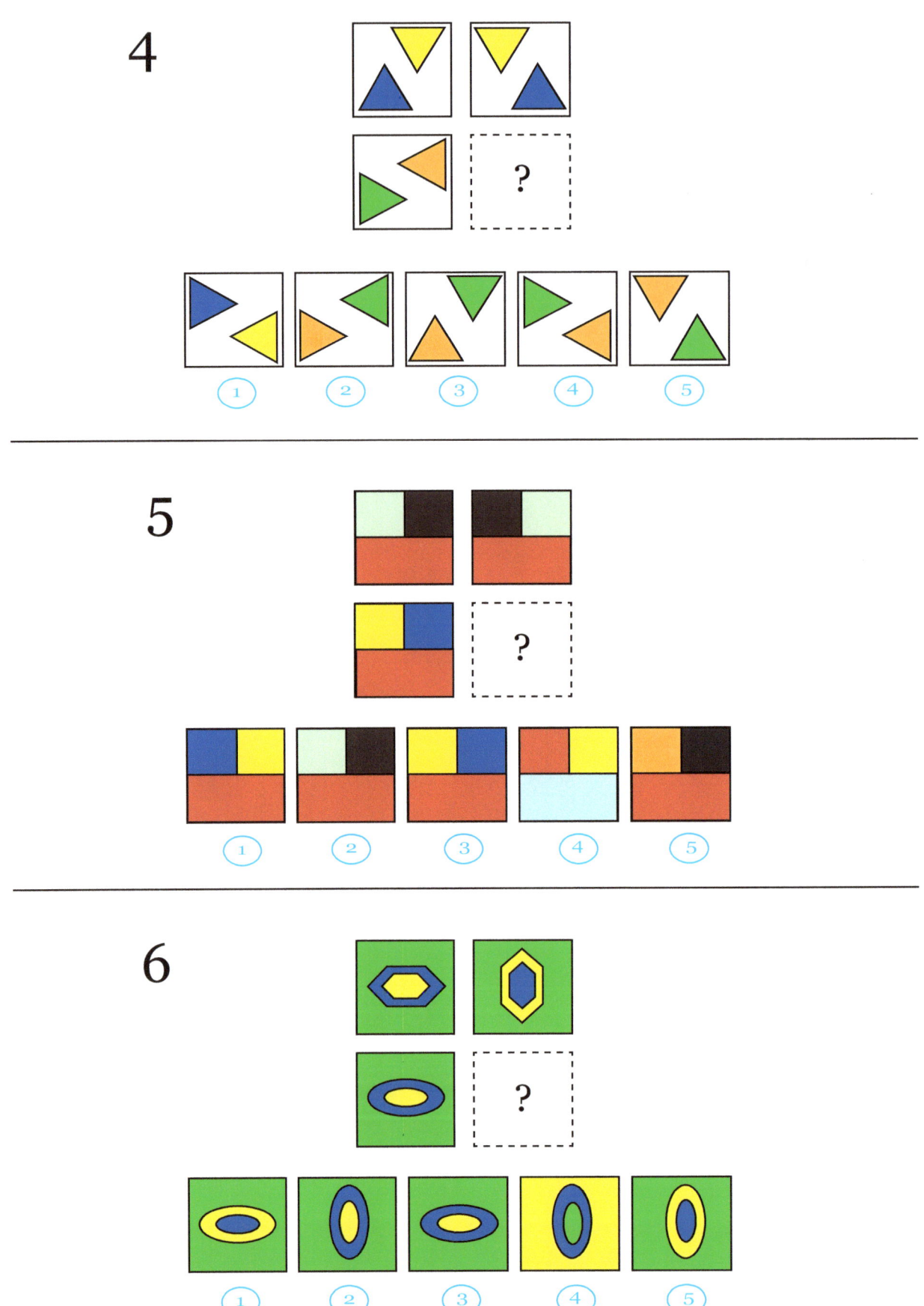

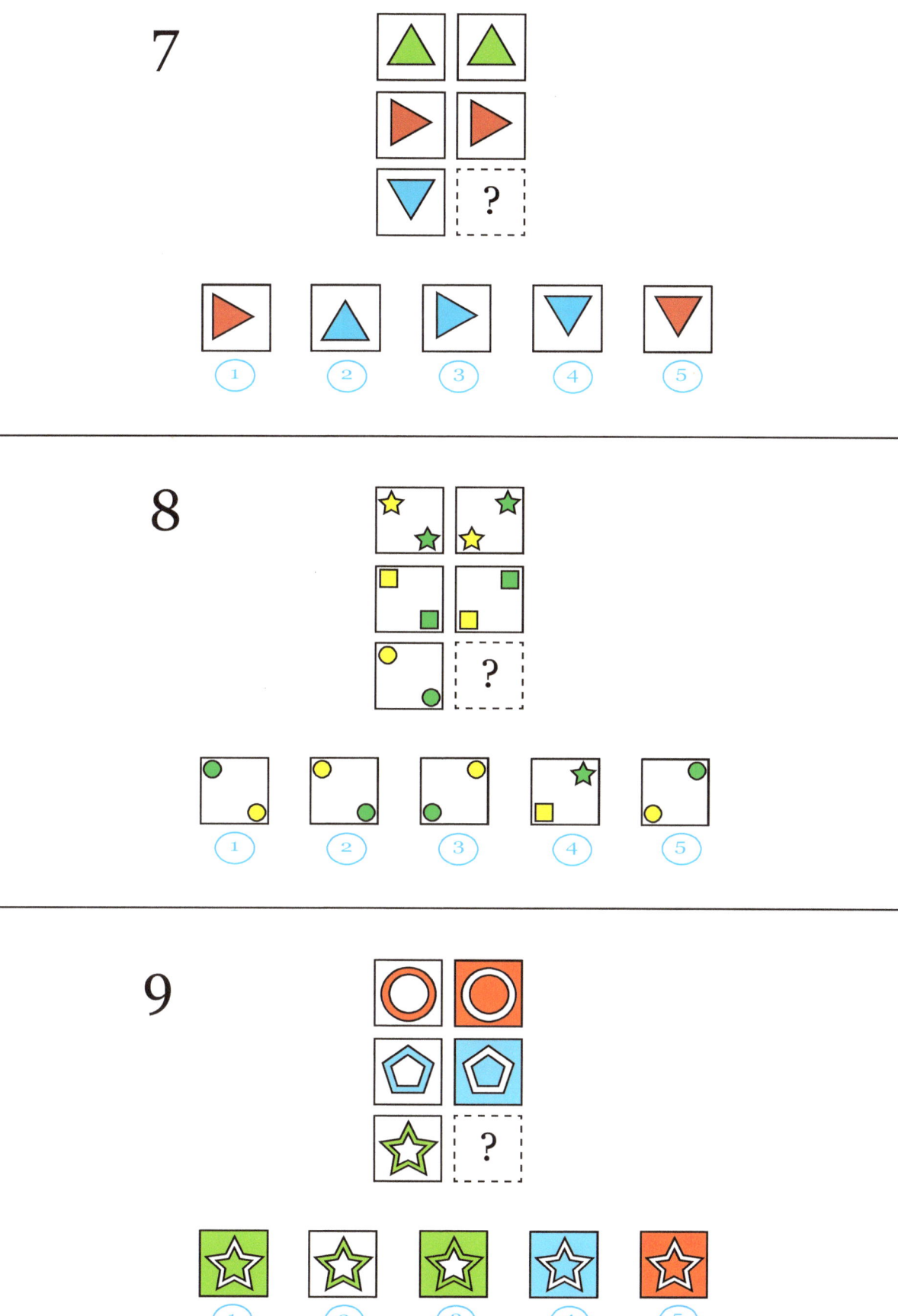

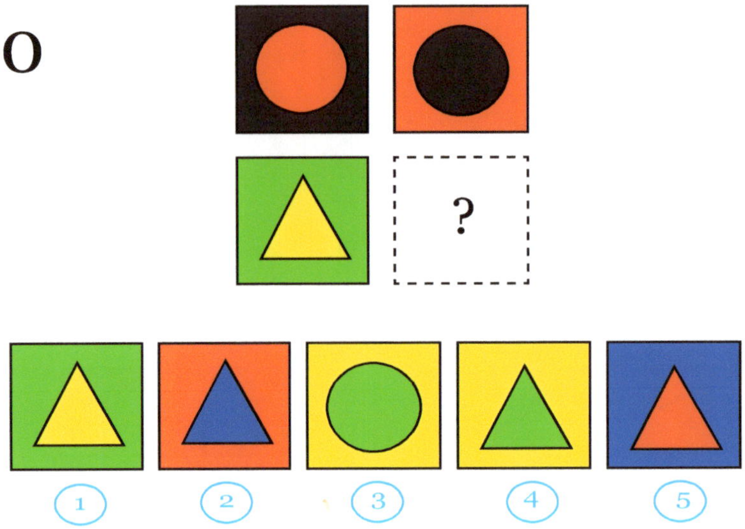

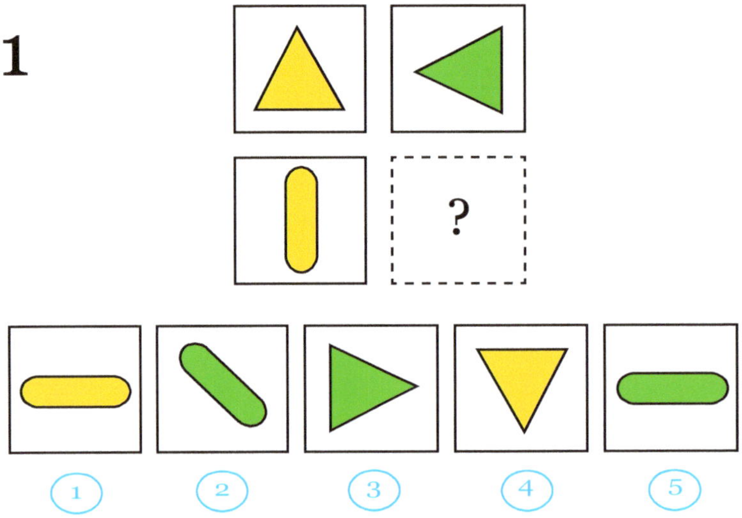

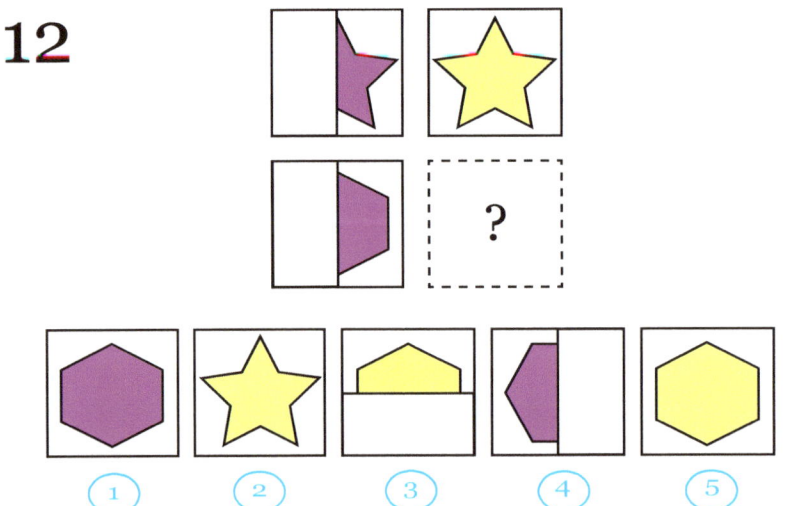

13

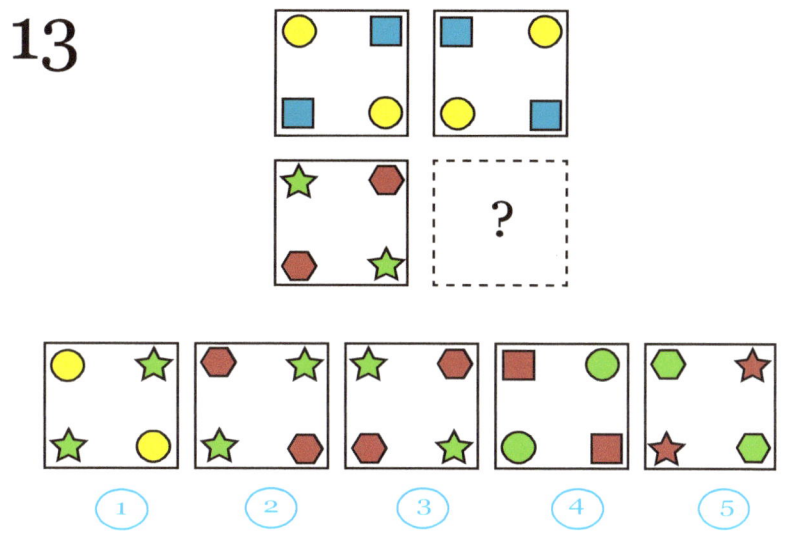

14

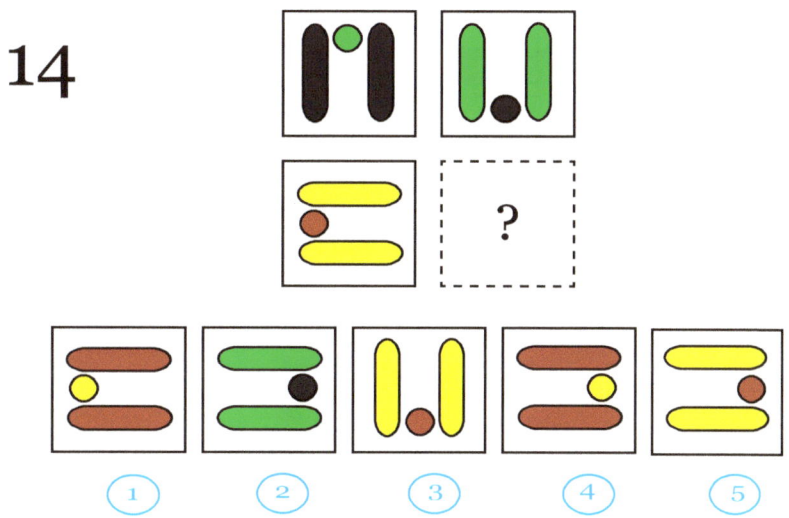

15

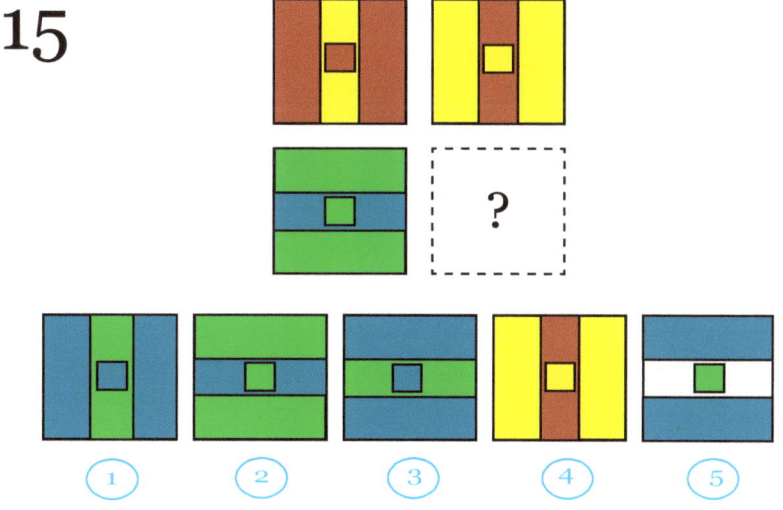

16

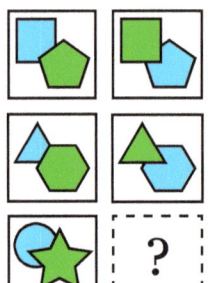

① ② ③ ④ ⑤

17

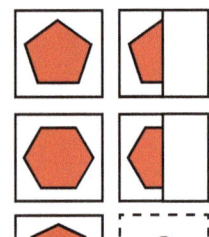

 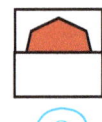   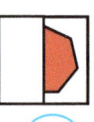
① ② ③ ④ ⑤

18

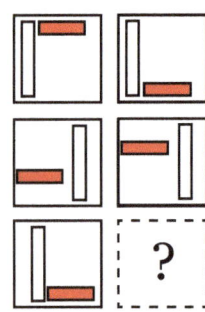

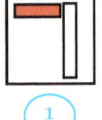 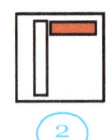   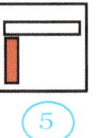
① ② ③ ④ ⑤

19

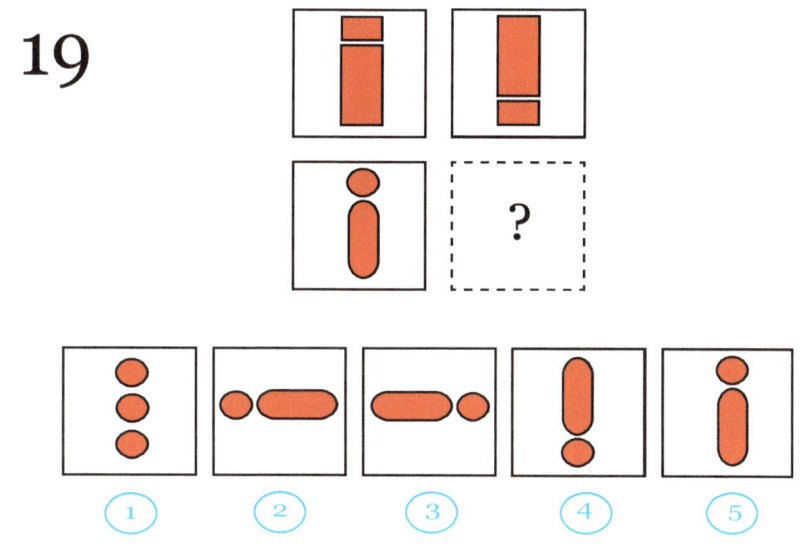

20

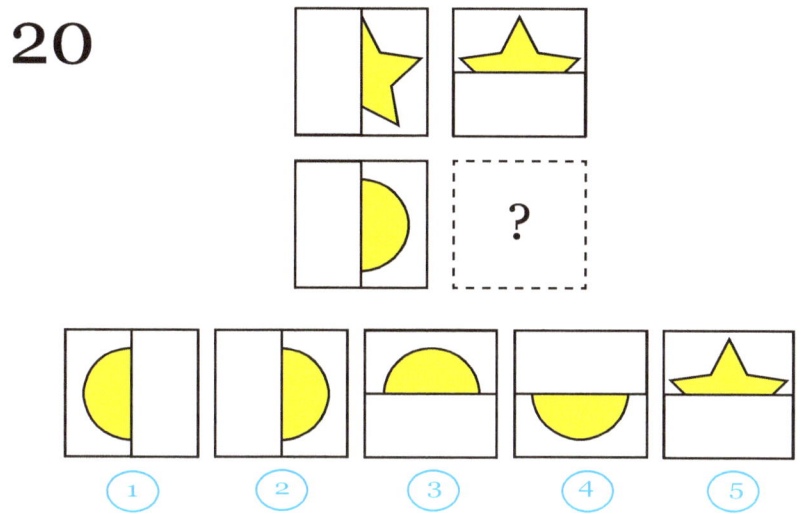

21

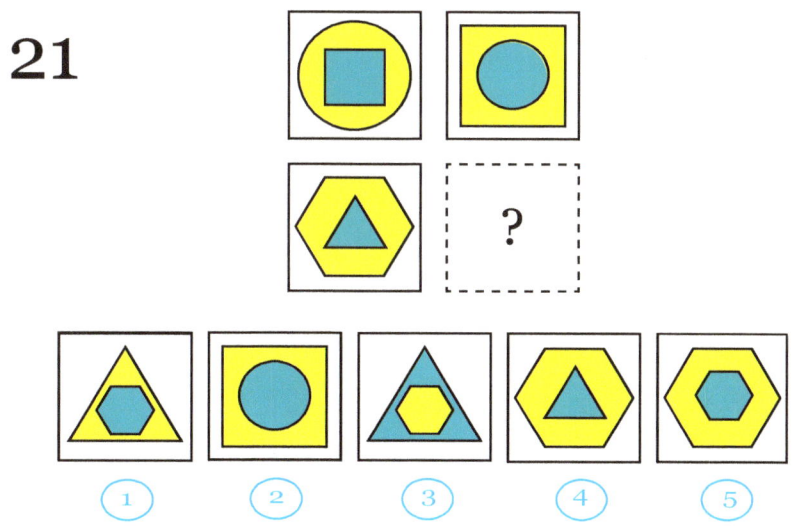

22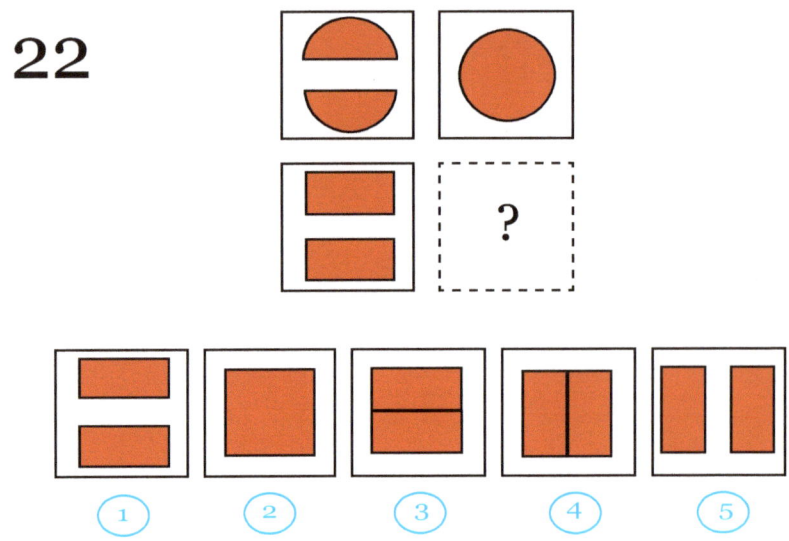

23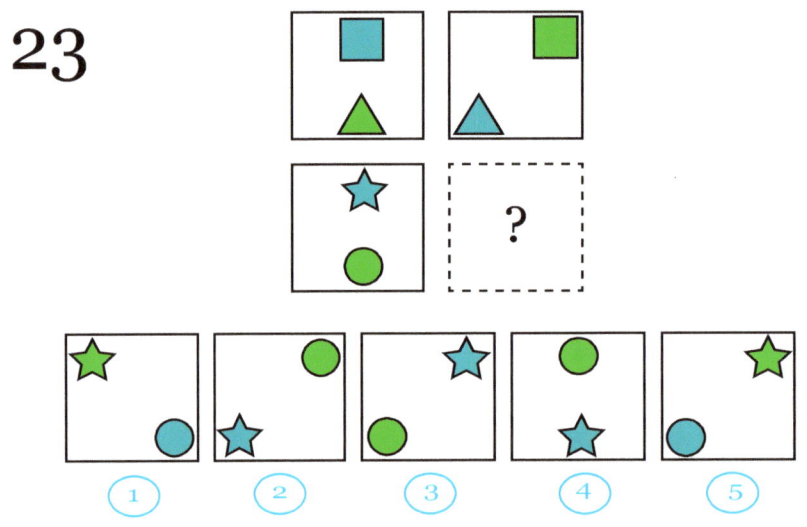

24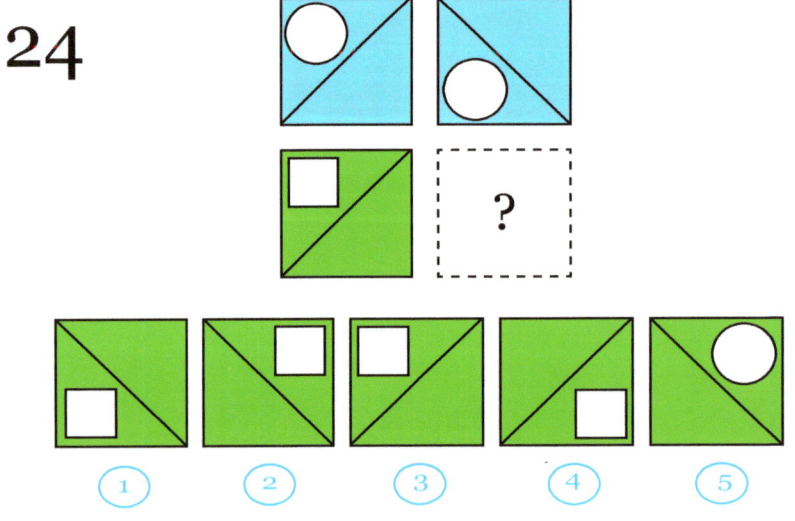

25

26

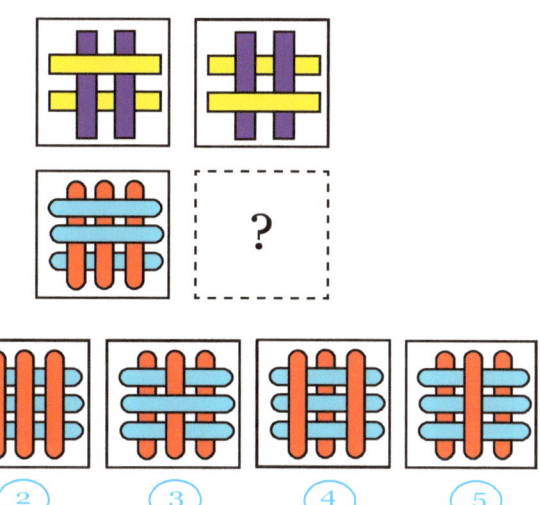

27

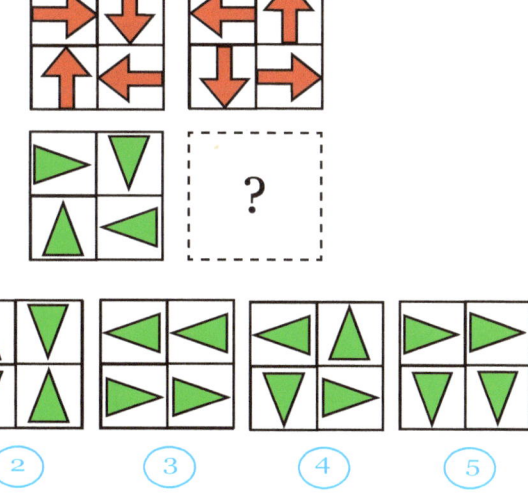

28

29

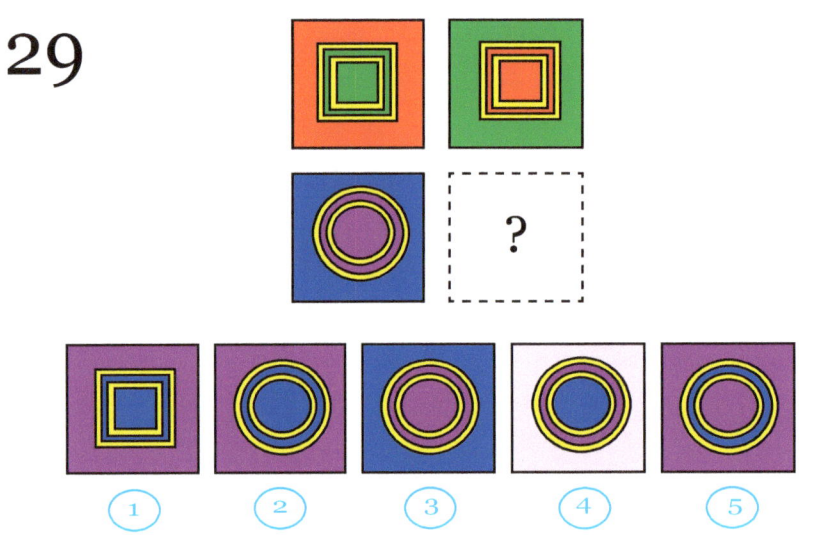

30

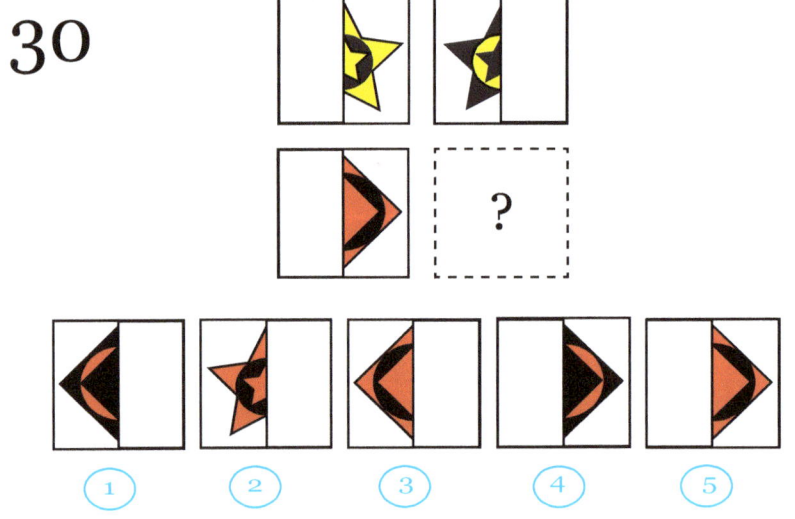

Serial Reasoning

With this question type, the student is shown a series of shapes that change across the rows and columns throughout the design. These questions require the child to understand how the objects in rows and columns relate to each other. The child must isolate and apply the rule/s in order to identify which object from the answer choices fits the empty box in the bottom right-hand corner of the matrix.

Before each question in this section, say to your child:

"Look at the picture. A piece is missing where you see the question mark. Show me the piece that is missing in the answer choices."

Tips and Strategies

Encourage your student to discover the pattern by looking in each direction.

- Horizontally across the rows. Ask: "How do the objects change in the first row? Do you see a pattern? Do the objects change in the same way in the second row? The third row?"
- Vertically down the columns. Ask: "How do the objects change in the first column? Do you see a pattern? Do the objects change in the same way in the second column? The third column?"
- Diagonally (if the item is a 6-box matrix). Ask: "How do the objects change across the diagonal? Do you see a pattern?"

Encourage your student to isolate one element (e.g: outer shape, inner shape/s) and identify how it changes.

- How does the color/shading of the element change as it moves along the row/column?
- Does the element change positions as it moves along the row/column? Does it move up, down or around (i.e.: clockwise, counter-clockwise). Does the element move to the opposite position?
- Does the element get bigger, smaller or stay the same as it moves?
- Does the element disappear and appear again as you move along the row/column?

1

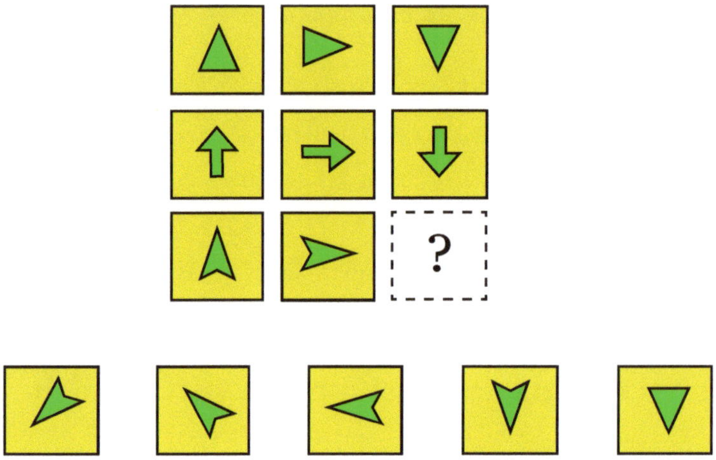

2

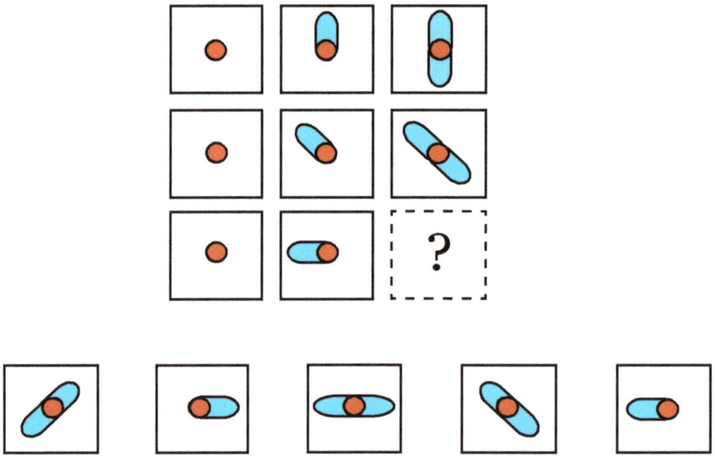

3

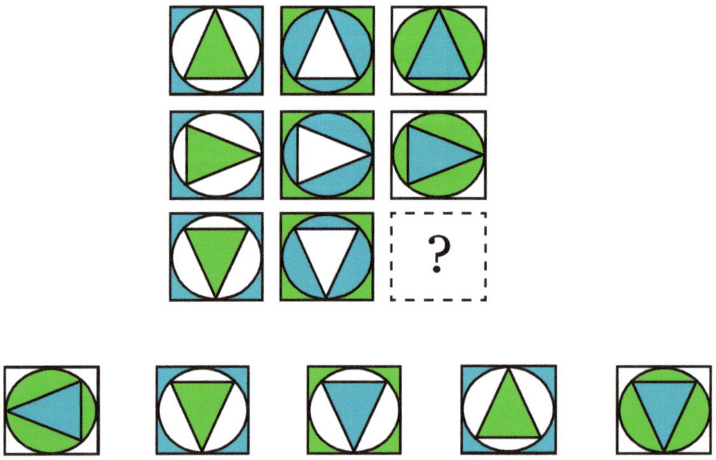

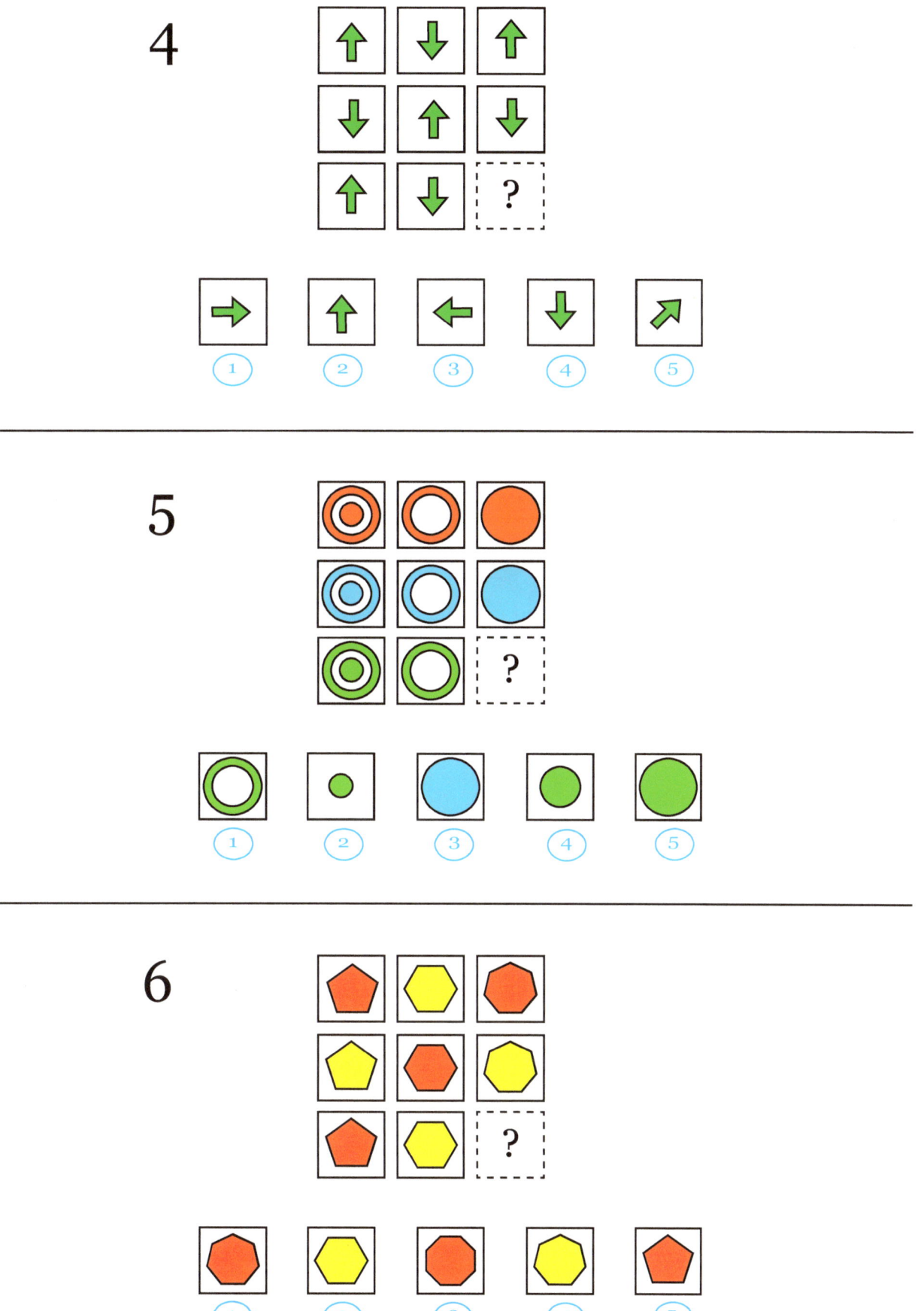

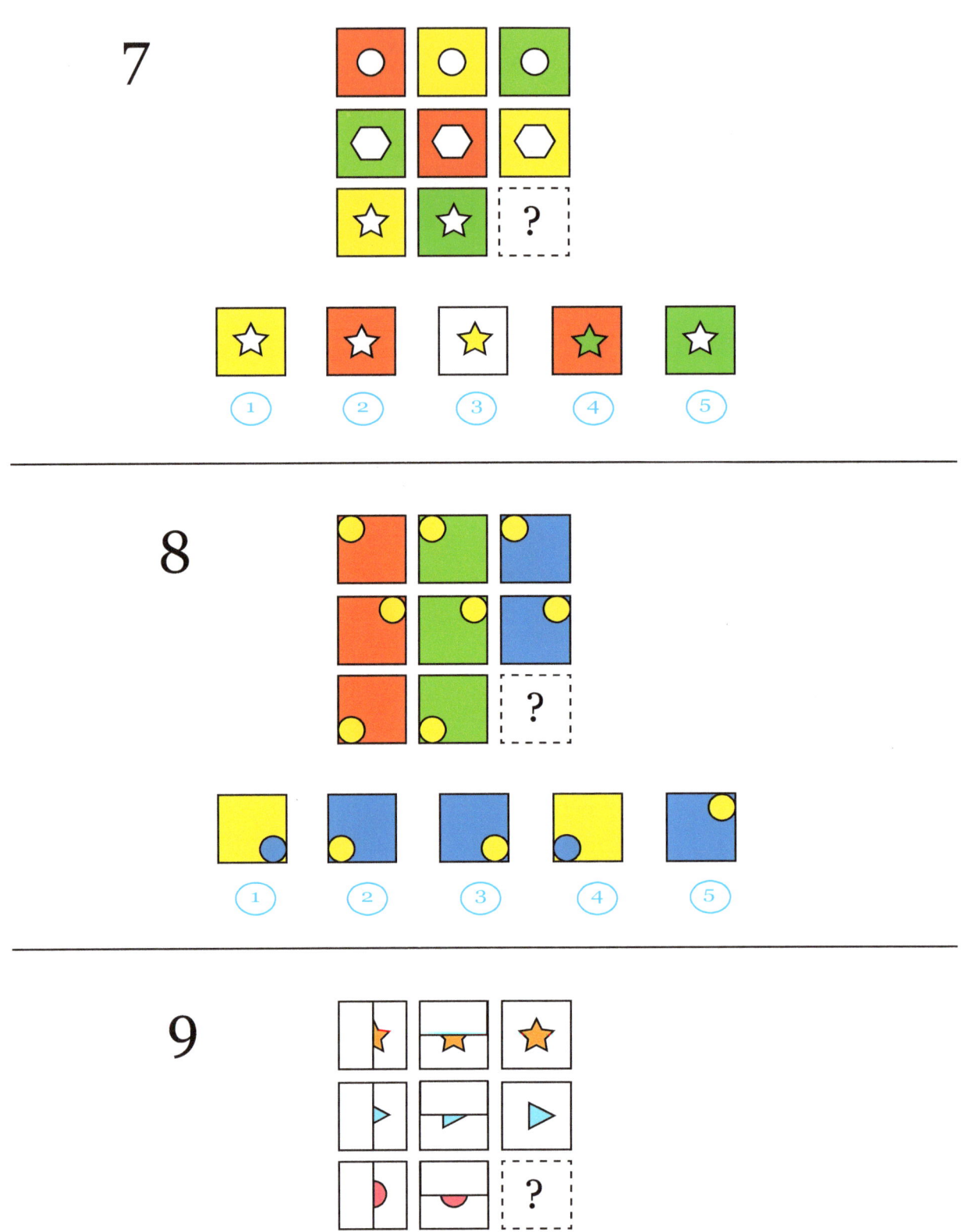

10

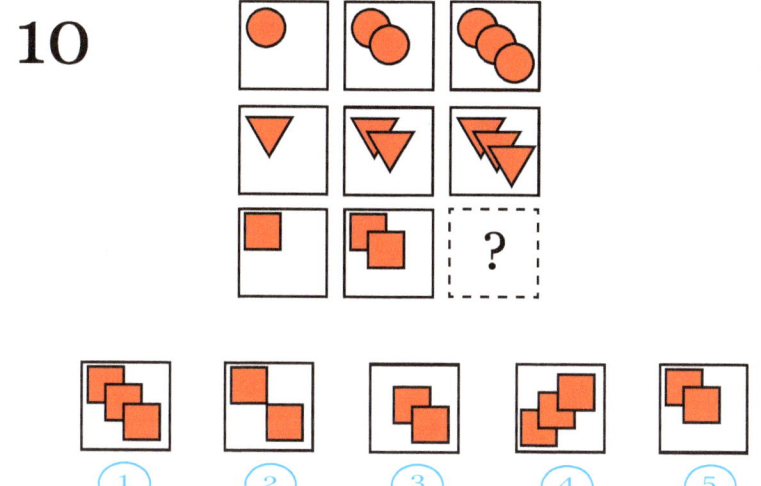

11

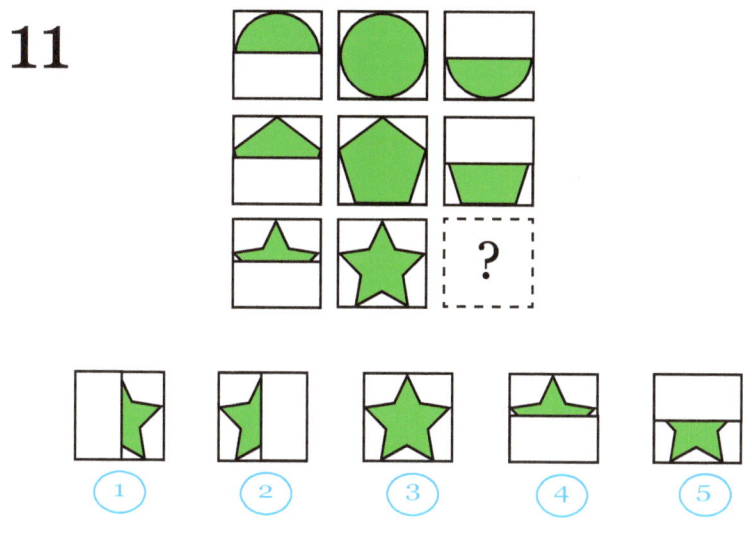

12

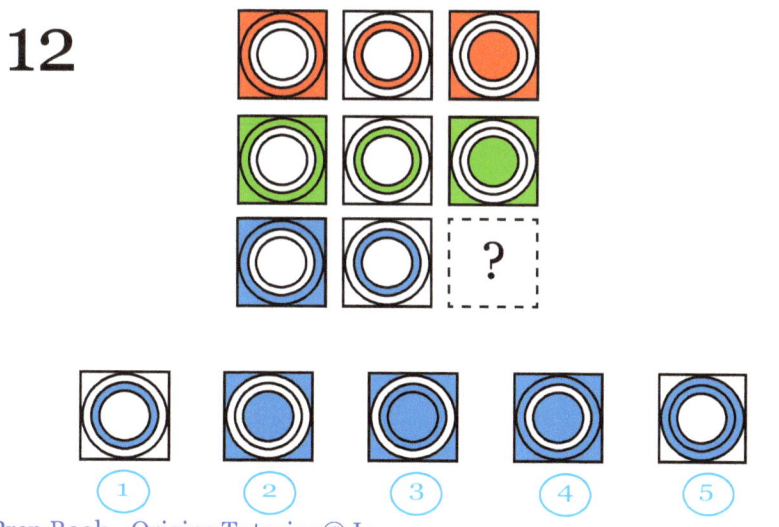

13

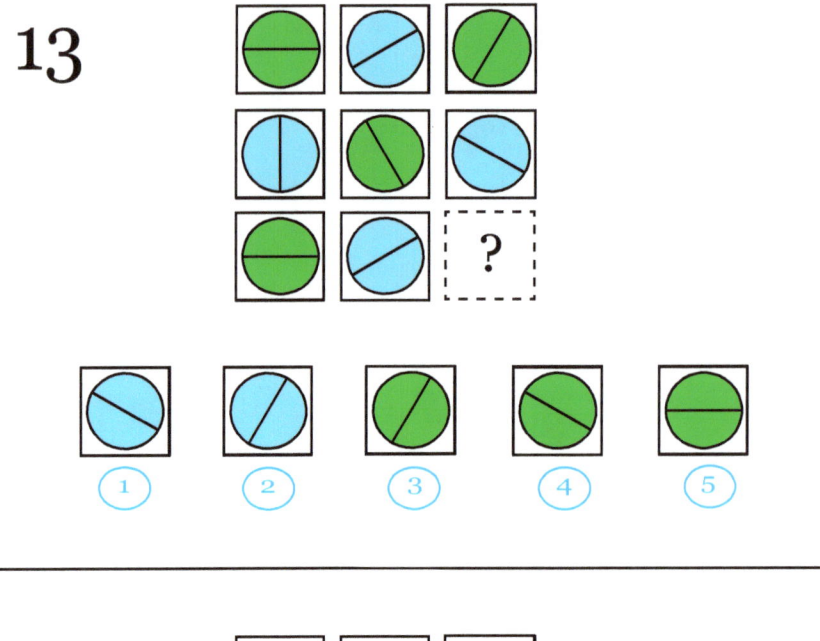

14

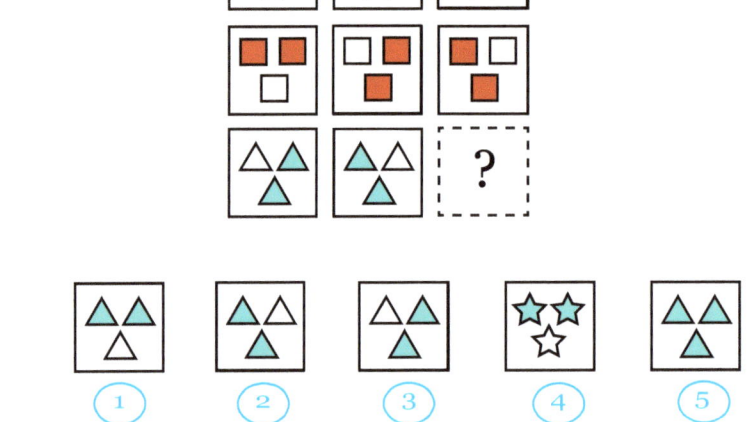

15

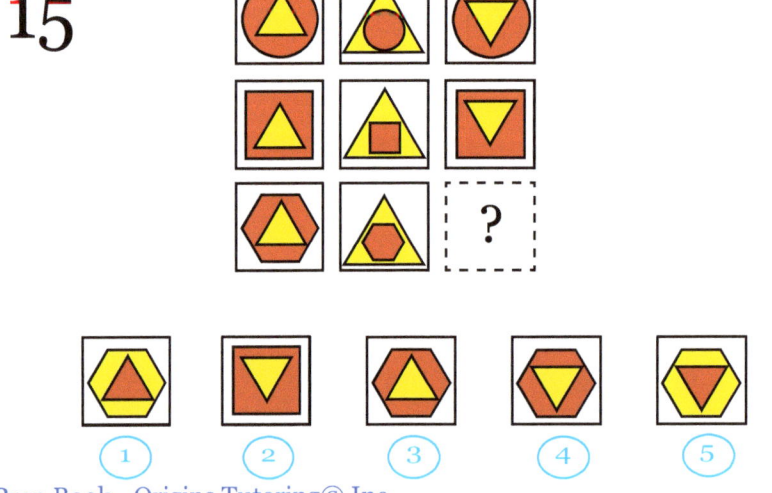

16

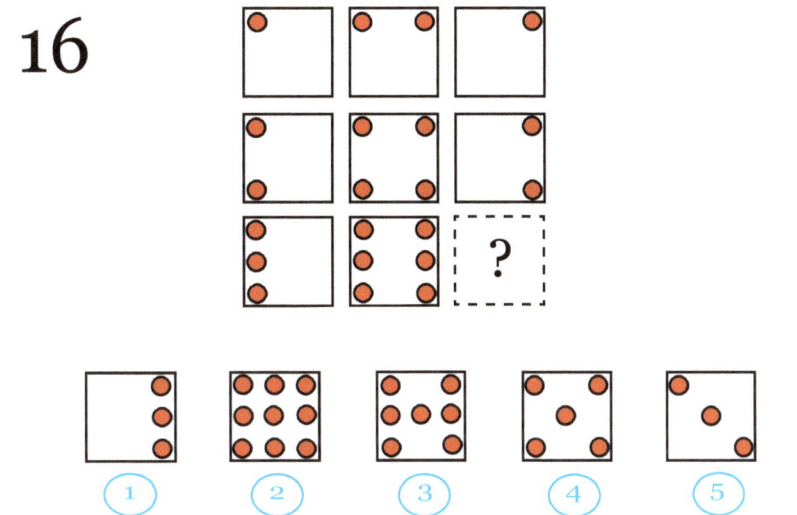

17

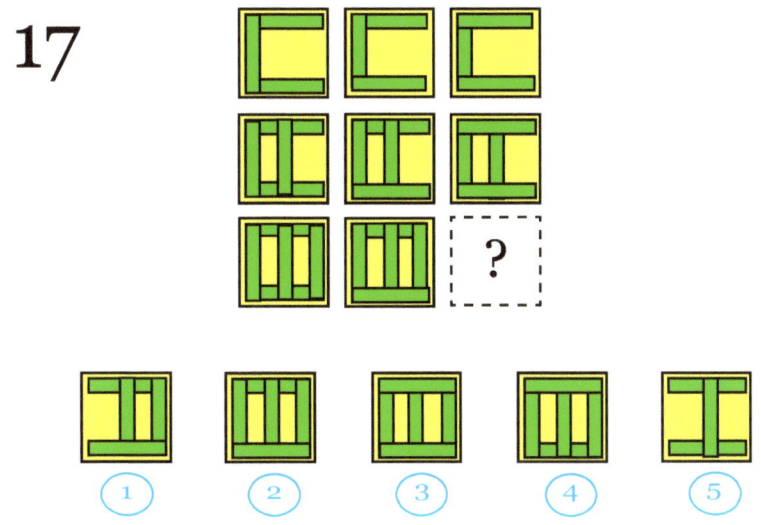

18

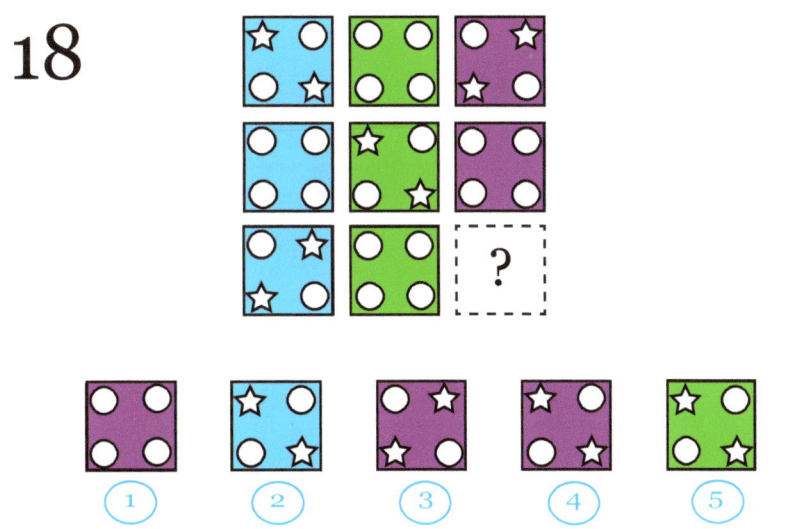

19

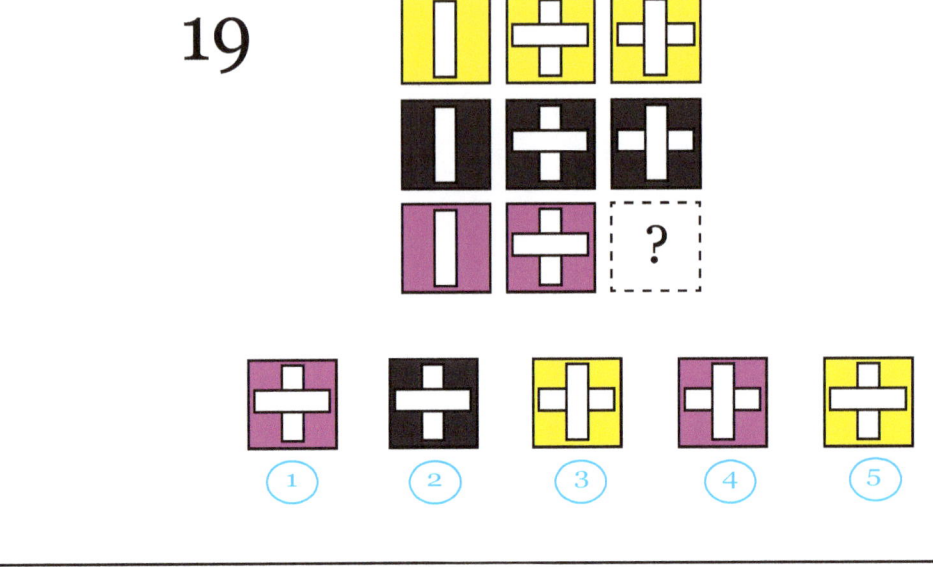

20

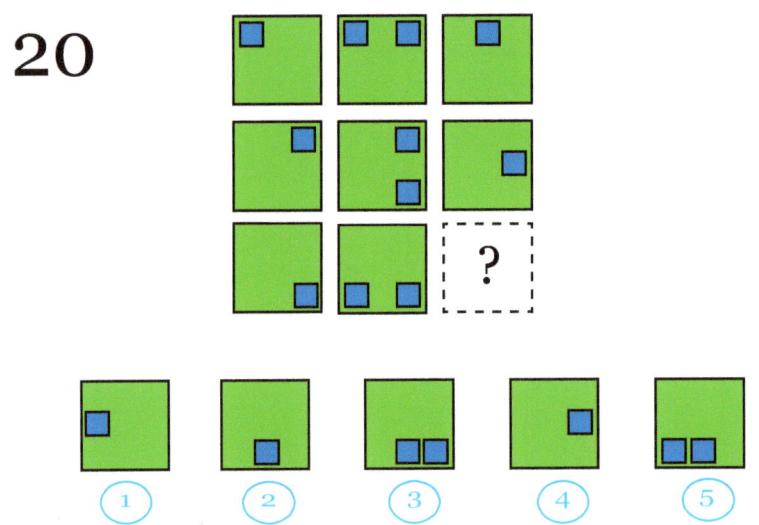

21

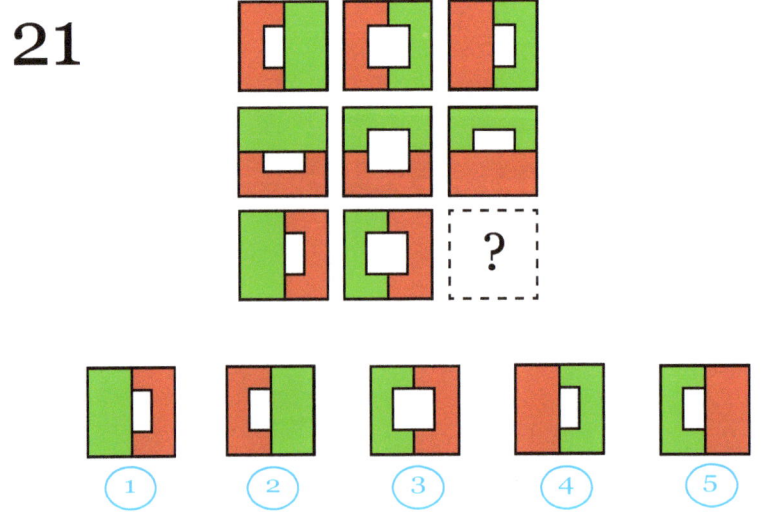

22

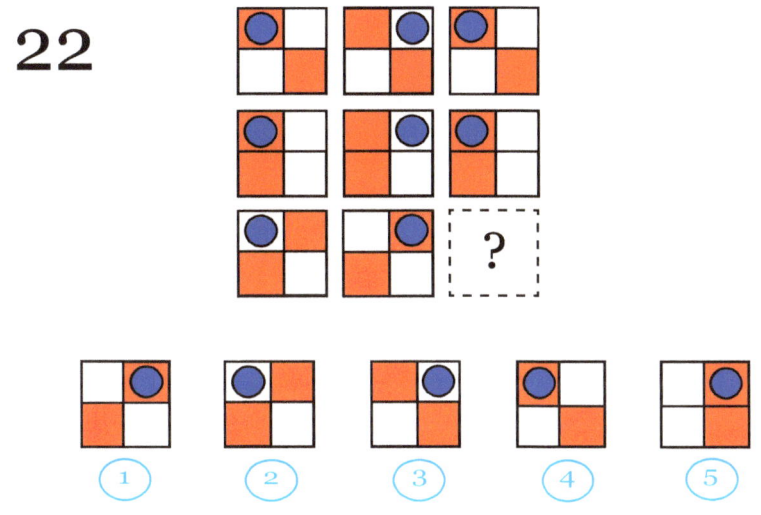

23

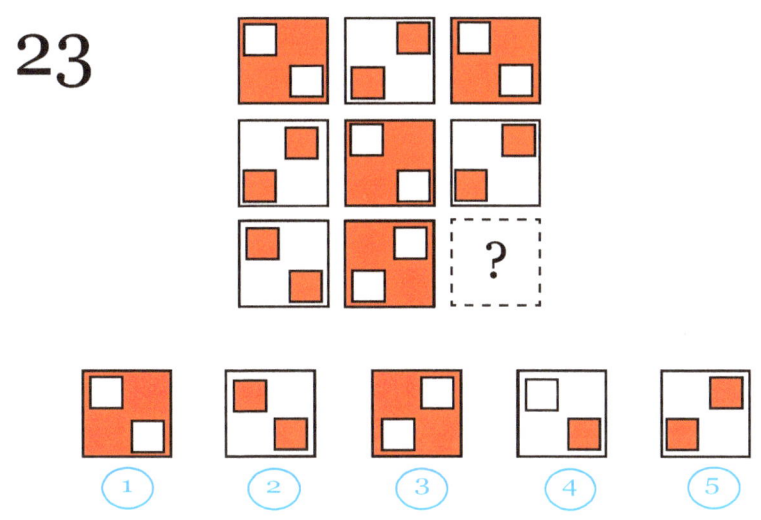

24

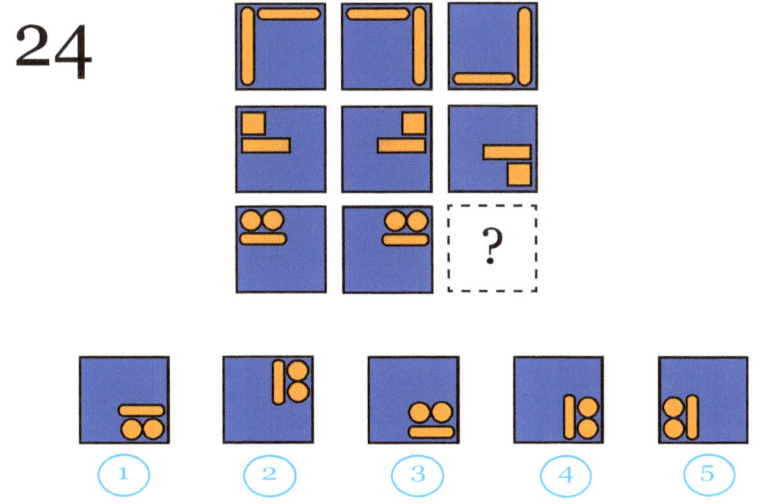

Answer Keys
NNAT®2/3
Skill-building Exercises

What Does Not Belong
What Does Not Belong

#	Ans
1.	4
2.	2
3.	1
4.	5
5.	2
6.	5
7.	1
8.	3
9.	5
10.	2
11.	4
12.	4
13.	5
14.	1
15.	4

Connecting and Taking Apart Shapes	
Connecting Shapes	Taking Apart Shapes
1. 1	1. 1 & 4
2. 2	2. 2 & 3
3. 4	3. 2 & 3
4. 3	4. 1 & 2
5. 2	5. 2 & 3
6. 4	6. 3 & 4
7. 1	7. 1 & 4
8. 4	8. 3 & 4
9. 3	9. 1 & 2
10. 3	10. 1 & 3
11. 2	11. 3 & 4
12. 4	12. 1 & 3
13. 1	13. 2 & 3
14. 2	14. 1 & 2
15. 4	15. 1 & 2

Puzzles and Patterns	
Finding a Puzzle Piece	Matching Patterns
1. 3	1. 2
2. 1	2. 3
3. 3	3. 1
4. 4	4. 3
5. 2	5. 2
6. 2	6. 1
7. 1	7. 2
8. 4	8. 4
9. 3	9. 4
10. 2	10. 3
11. 2	11. 1
12. 4	12. 2
13. 1	13. 3
14. 3	14. 3
15. 4	15. 2

Sequences
Sequences

#	Ans
1.	4
2.	1
3.	2
4.	2
5.	3
6.	2
7.	1
8.	4
9.	3

Answer Key
NNAT®2/3 Practice Questions

Pattern Completion Questions	
1.	4
2.	2
3.	3
4.	5
5.	1
6.	3
7.	2
8.	4
9.	5
10.	3
11.	1
12.	4
13.	2
14.	5
15.	2
16.	3
17.	5
18.	3
19.	4
20.	1
21.	5
22.	4
23.	3
24.	4
25.	3
26.	2
27.	2
28.	5
29.	4
30.	3
31.	2
32.	5
33.	1
34.	5
35.	3
36.	2

Reasoning by Analogy Questions	
1.	3
2.	5
3.	2
4.	4
5.	1
6.	5
7.	4
8.	5
9.	1
10.	4
11.	5
12.	5
13.	2
14.	4
15.	3
16.	3
17.	3
18.	2
19.	4
20.	3
21.	1
22.	2
23.	5
24.	1
25.	4
26.	1
27.	4
28.	2
29.	2
30.	1

Serial Reasoning Questions	
1.	4
2.	3
3.	5
4.	2
5.	5
6.	1
7.	2
8.	2
9.	5
10.	1
11.	5
12.	2
13.	3
14.	1
15.	4
16.	1
17.	3
18.	4
19.	4
20.	2
21.	5
22.	2
23.	2
24.	1

OLSAT® Practice Questions

The OLSAT part of the NYC Gifted and Talented test is comprised of three different question types:

1. **Following Directions**
2. **Aural Reasoning**
3. **Arithmetic Reasoning**

This section of the book features practice questions for all these question types. The practice questions for each question type are divided into separate chapters.

Please note that in an official OLSAT® test, the test questions are presented in random order and are not divided up. This means that there will not be specific sections with questions only on "Following Directions" or "Aural Reasoning".

Before your student attempts the practice questions, we recommend that you spend a few minutes yourself reviewing the teaching tips for each section so you can be prepared to help your student if he or she struggles with a question.

Please note that on the official test. a student will be allowed to hear a question one time ONLY. The one-time reading of the question is strictly enforced in the exam room because the test is measuring how well your child comprehends and retains information, and reading the question once is one way in which the test assesses this skill.

Keep in mind that when your child is first exposed to practice questions in a new section, you may need to repeat information. As your child improves his 'listening' skills and becomes more confident, we suggest you ask the question just one time.

Remember to download the OLSAT® practice test at www.originstutoring.com/bonus-test-14

Following Directions

'Following Directions' questions measure a student's ability to listen carefully and choose a representation (figural design or picture) of a description that is read to a student by a test administrator.

- These questions test a student's knowledge of relational concepts, including distinguishing between and understanding phrases such as "up", "down", "below", "above", "behind" and "next to."

- These questions test knowledge of sizes, shapes, numbers, and letters.

- These questions measure a student's understanding of concepts such as neither/nor, and the order of things, such as first, second, third, etc.

In this section, you will find **25 "Following Directions"** practice questions to help your student learn the concepts and practice the skills necessary to perform successfully on the official OLSAT® exam.

Tips and Strategies

- Make sure your student is focused by asking her to **"listen carefully"** before each question.

- Tell your student to **look at the answer options** while you read the questions. Ask your student to **eliminate obviously wrong answers** to narrow down the answer choices.

- Ask your student to **explain why she chose a specific answer**. If the answer was incorrect, this will help you identify where your student is stumbling. If the answer was correct, asking your student to articulate her reasoning will help reinforce her understanding of a concept.

Following Directions

1. The picture at the beginning of the row shows an apple pie, a birthday cake and a pizza. Josie and her friends ate half the pizza, half of the apple pie but none of the birthday cake. Which picture shows what was leftover at the end?

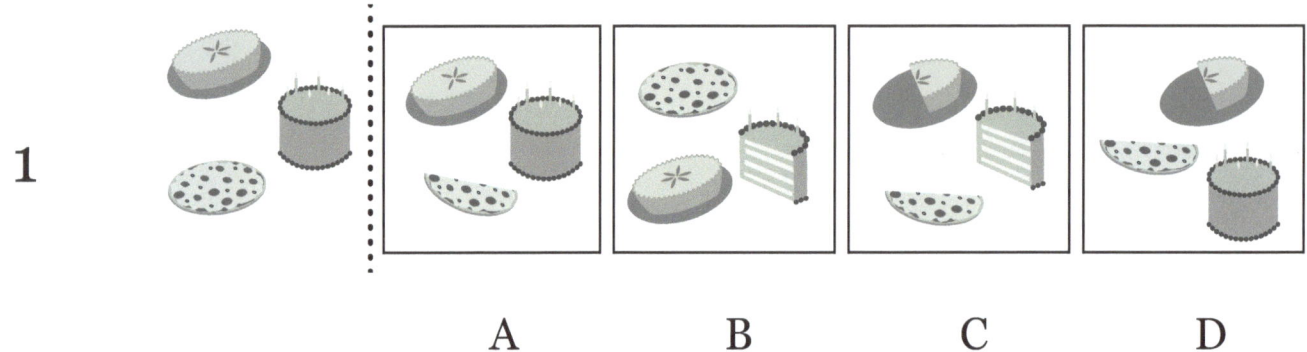

A B C D

2. At the beginning of the row you can see a box with letters, numbers and shapes. Which picture shows the shape above the letter A and below the number 2?

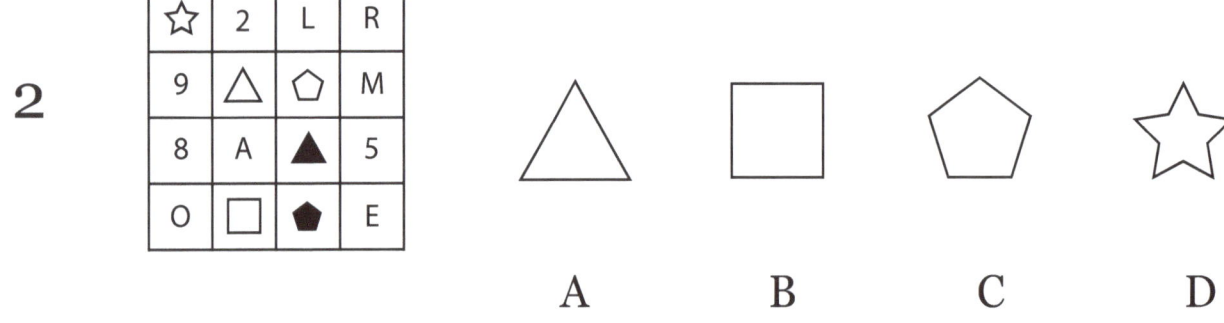

A B C D

3. Which picture shows three flowers in a vase and a hand ready to put one more flower in the vase?

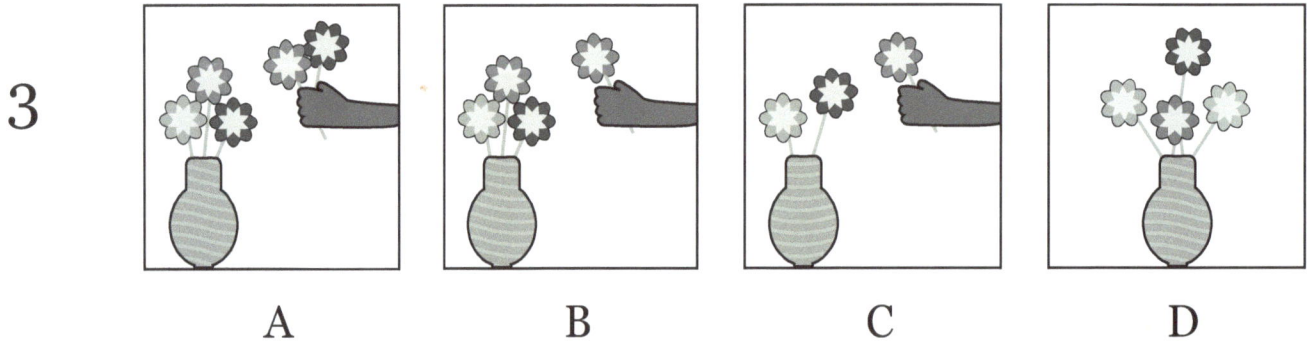

A B C D

Following Directions

Which picture shows this: There are three striped stars inside of a white square?

4

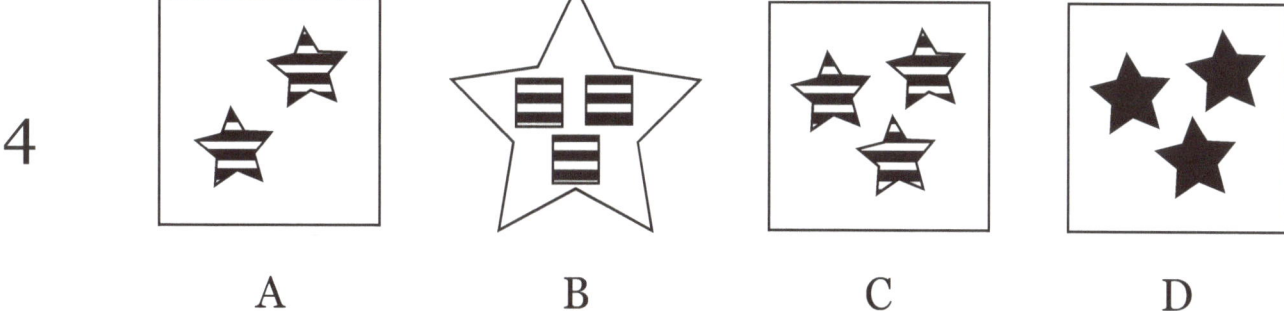

A B C D

Charlotte likes going to the playground and playing on the slide, swinging on the swing, and climbing on the jungle gym. Which picture shows all the things Charlotte likes to do when she goes to the playground?

5

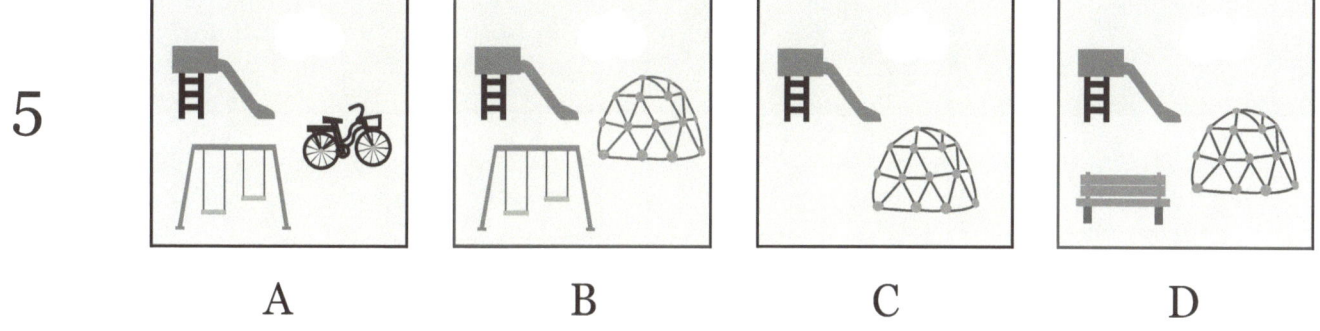

A B C D

Which picture shows a girl jumping over a puddle, and a boy standing next to a boy clapping?

6

A B C D

Following Directions

When Kate gets ready for bed, she first brushes her teeth. Then, she changes into her pajamas. Next, she kisses her teddy bear. Last, she reads a book. Which picture shows the third activity that Kate does when she gets ready for bed?

7

A   B   C   D

Which picture shows a bird above a tree and a bird below a tree?

8

A   B   C   D

Sarah is having a tea party with her friends. First, she puts out plates, then cups, then spoons and finally the napkins on the table. Which picture shows the second thing she put out on the table?

9

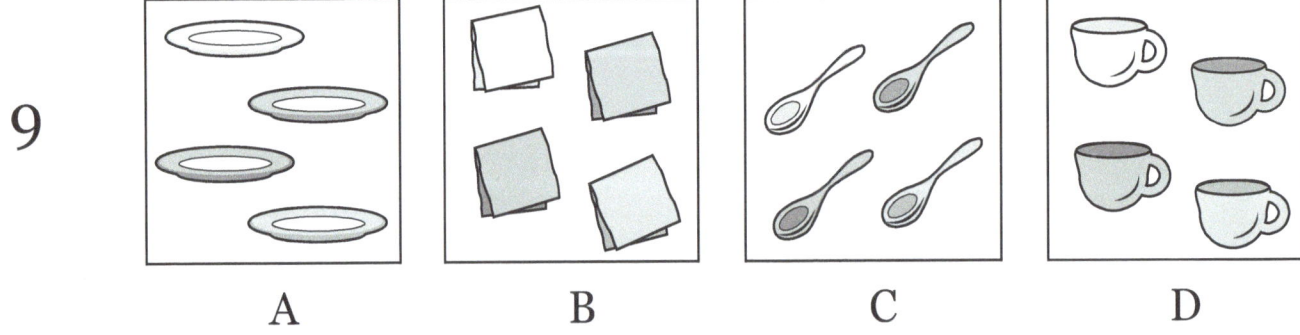

A   B   C   D

Following Directions

Which picture shows a circle inside of a triangle on top of a black heart?

10

    A   B   C   D

In the row below, you can see pictures of some toys. Which picture has neither a teddy bear nor a soccer ball in it?

11

    A   B   C   D

At the beginning of the row you can see a box with letters, numbers and shapes. Which picture shows the shape below the letter V?

12

    A   B   C   D

Following Directions

Which picture shows a white heart between a gray heart and a small gray square?

13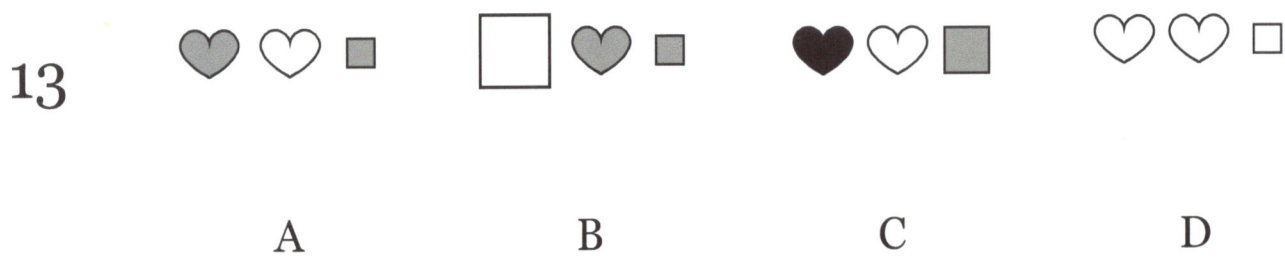

    A   B   C   D

In the Evans family, Ron is younger than Bella, and Mia is older than both Ron and Bella. Which picture shows the Evans family?

14

    A   B   C   D

Which picture shows a white star on top of a striped square above a large striped triangle?

15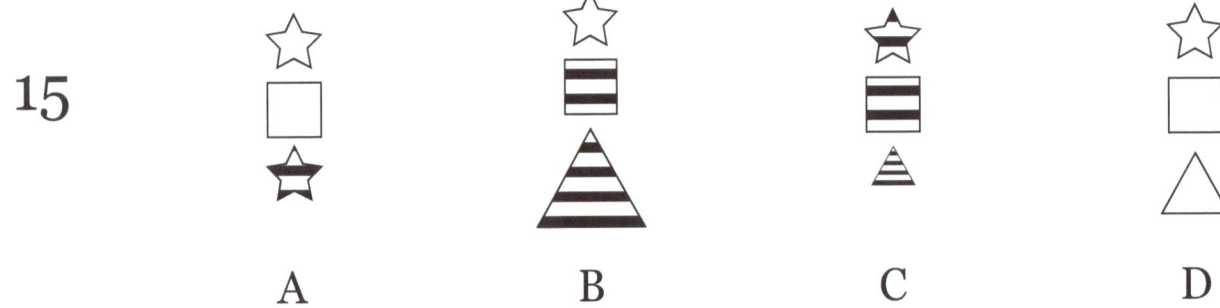

    A   B   C   D

Following Directions

Which picture shows four squares next to each other and a triangle on top of the first and last square?

16

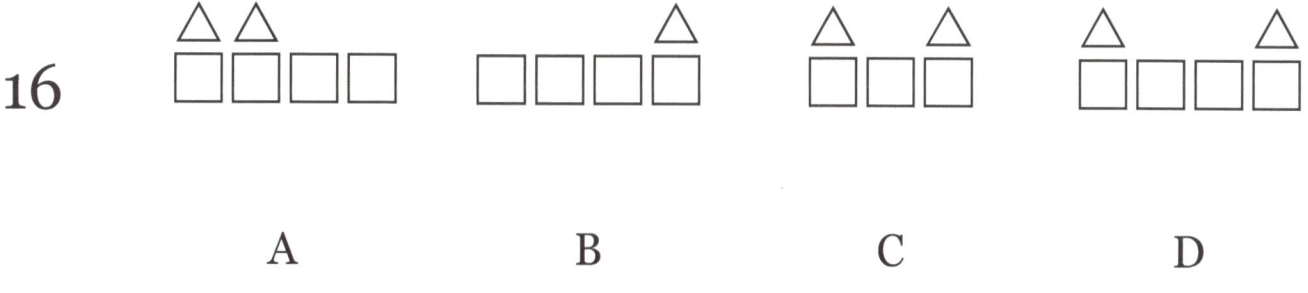

A B C D

Which picture shows a white pig and a black sheep among all the animals?

17

A B C D

Which picture show this: Jack is kicking a black and white ball. He is wearing a white cap, and has a t-shirt and long pants on.

18

A B C D

Following Directions

Which picture shows two small black pigs between a large striped pig and a white sheep?

19   A   B   C   D

Which picture shows two frogs in the pond and three frogs next to the pond?

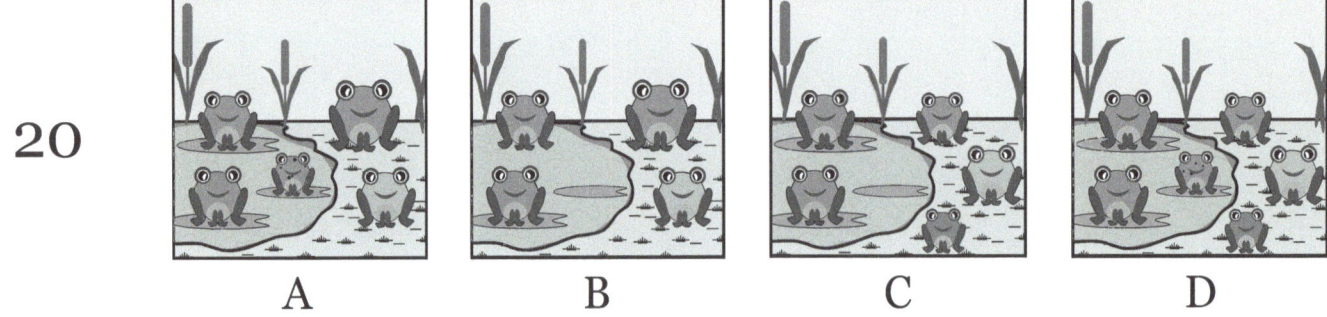

20   A   B   C   D

Sasha does her chores everyday. Which picture shows Sasha sweeping the floor with a black broom between a lamp and a sofa.?

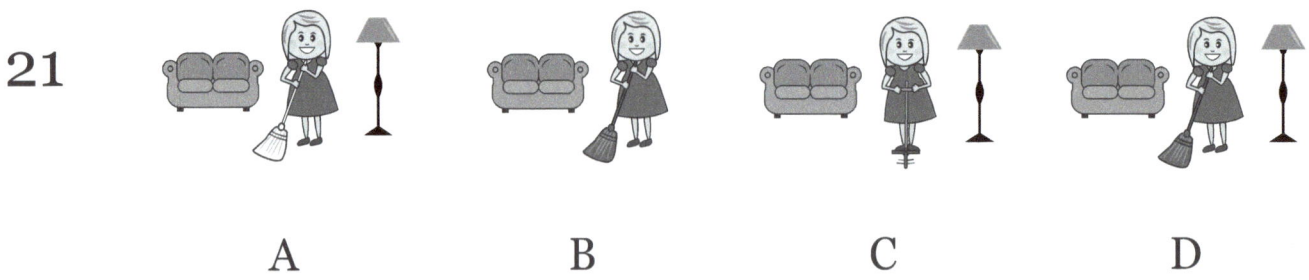

21   A   B   C   D

Following Directions

Paul's mother makes lemonade. She pours a full glass for herself and a half glass each for Paul and his friend, Lewis. Which picture shows what Paul's mother poured?

22

A    B    C    D

Maggie is typing on her computer. She types first the letter X, then the letter Z, then the letter Y, and then the letter W. Which picture shows what Maggie sees on her computer screen?

23   ZYXW   XZYW   XWYZ   WXYZ

A   B   C   D

Which picture shows one horse in the stable and two horses in the field next to a fence?

24

A    B    C    D

Following Directions

Three children are buying ice cream. Which picture shows the tallest girl third in line and the two shortest children at the front of the line?

25

A   B   C   D

Aural Reasoning

'Aural Reasoning' questions assess a student's ability to listen to, understand and visualize a question that is read aloud to him or her. These questions assess listening skills, visual vocabulary, and understanding about the characteristics and functions of things. They also measure the ability to pay close attention to details, and the ability to use logic and inferences to figure out the correct outcome and response.

In this section, you will find **20 "Aural Reasoning"** practice questions to help your student learn the concepts and practice the skills necessary to perform successfully on the official OLSAT® exam..

Tips and Strategies

- Make sure your student is focused by asking him to **"listen carefully"** before each question.

- Tell your student to **look at the answer options** while you ask the questions. Ask your student to **eliminate obviously wrong answers** to narrow down the answer choices.

- Ask your student to **explain why he chose a specific answer**. This will help you identify where your student is stumbling, and be an opportunity to reinforce his understanding of the concept and/or calculation.

- If your student consistently cannot recall all the information read aloud to her in these questions, **leave out some details that are not essential**. Gradually add in more information when you think your student is ready. Aim ultimately to read the whole question just once, as this reflects the actual testing environment.

Aural Reasoning

Ramona has three pets. Ramona's cat weighs more than her lizard, and her hamster weighs more than her lizard. Which picture shows the pet that weighs the least?

1

A B C D

Zack was at the beach playing in the ocean with his friends. He asked his mother to bring him something to help him float in the water. Which picture shows what his mother bought him?

2

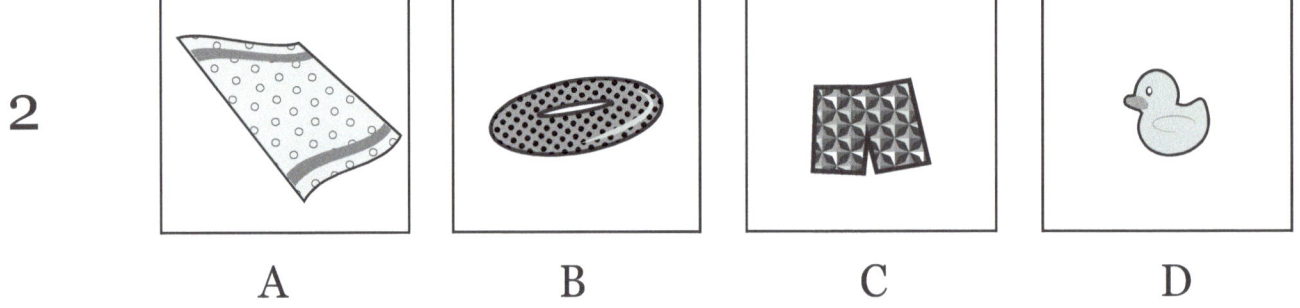

A B C D

Which picture shows a person who is neither riding a bike nor swimming?

3

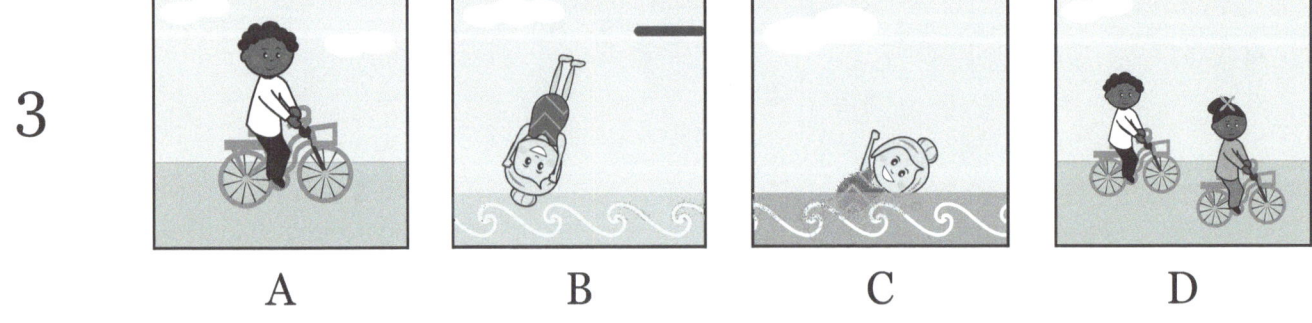

A B C D

Aural Reasoning

Margaret has a black teddy bear with grey paws and a gray bow tie. Paul's teddy bear looks the opposite of Margaret's. Which picture shows Paul's teddy bear?

4

    A   B   C   D

Max decides to plant some seeds in a flower pot. First he digs a hole in the earth. Then he sprinkles the seeds in the hole and then he pours water in the pot. He looks at the pot again in a few days. Which picture shows what he saw?

5

    A   B   C   D

Lucas has one black bag and two white bags. Frank also has three bags, but he does not have white bags. Which picture shows Frank's bags?

6

 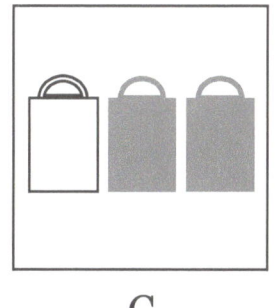 

    A   B   C   D

Aural Reasoning

Sandy was in her room with her friend Angeline. Sandy wanted to listen to some music, but Angeline did not. Which picture shows what Sandy used to listen to music?

7

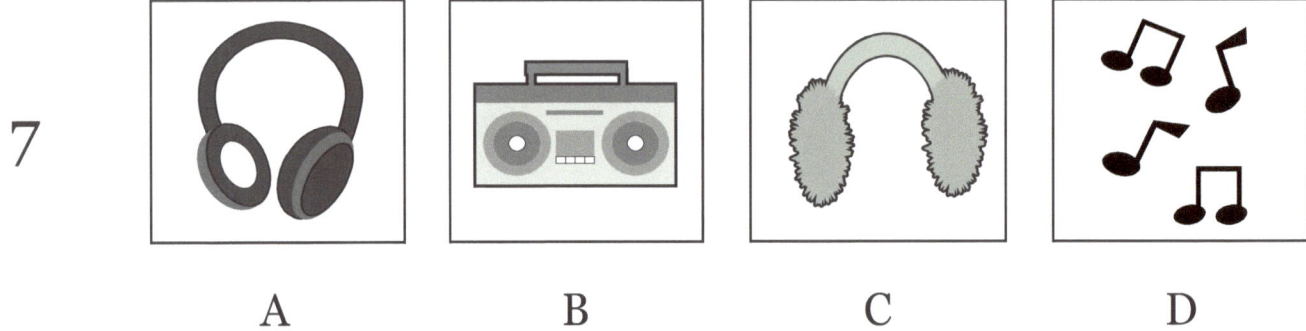

A   B   C   D

Isla and Melodie both play instruments. Isla plays instruments with strings. Melodie plays the same instruments as Isla, but she also plays the flute. Which picture shows what Melodie plays?

8

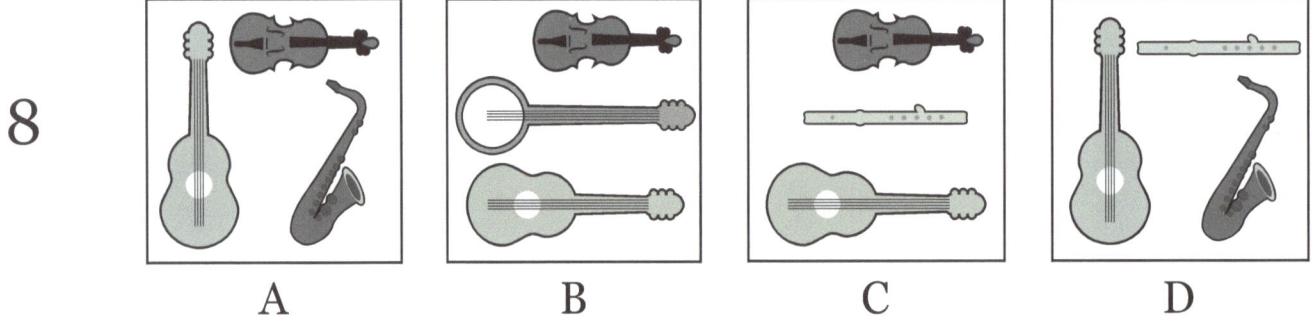

A   B   C   D

Bessie decided to make a sandcastle at the beach. First she gathered a pile of sand. Then, she put the sand in her bucket with her shovel. Then she used the bucket to make a sandcastle, then the sea came in and washed the sandcastle away. Which picture shows what Bessie did first?

9

A   B   C   D

Aural Reasoning

Brianna made a jug of lemonade for her friends. Her friends said they wished the lemonade was colder. What did Brianna put in the jug of lemonade to make it colder?

10 A B C D

Laura wanted to wear something fancy with buttons on it for her birthday. Which picture shows what Laura wore on her birthday?

11 A B C D

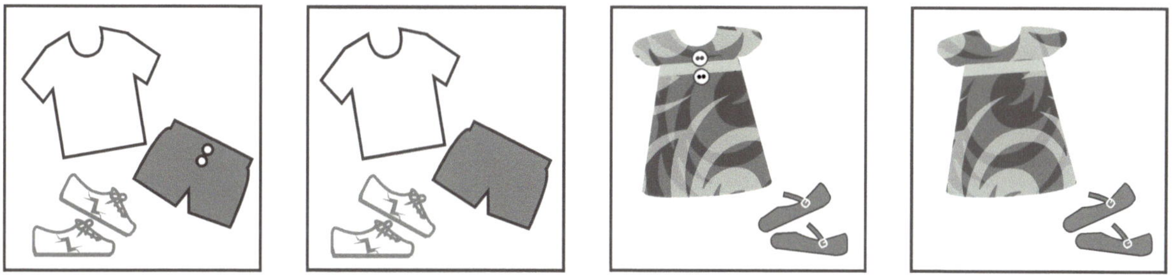

Lily's favorite fruits are fruits that can be peeled. Lily bought some fruits from the store and put them in a basket. Which picture shows Lily's favorite fruits?

12 A B C D

Aural Reasoning

Alan's mother told him that the flowers in the garden needed water. Which picture shows what Alan used to water the flowers?

13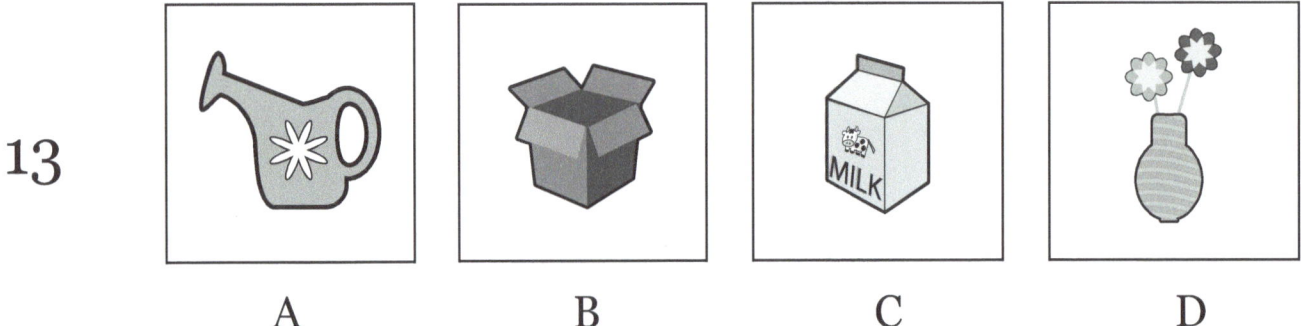

    A   B   C   D

A dog, a cow and a mouse were hungry. The dog wanted to eat meat. The cow wanted to eat grass. The mouse wanted to eat some cheese. Which picture shows what the cow wanted to do?

14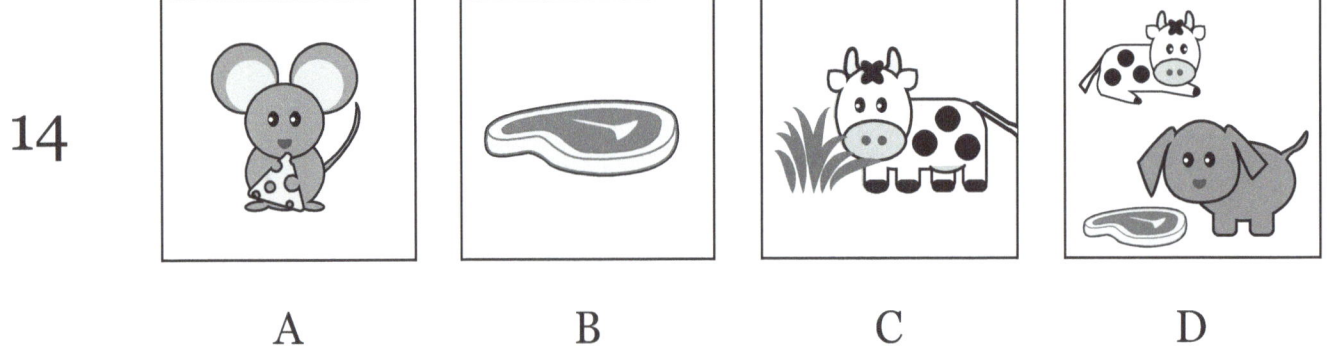

    A   B   C   D

Brian wanted to help his dad make dinner. Brian's dad told Brian to give him something so he would not burn his hand when putting the pan in the oven. Which picture shows what Brian bought his dad?

15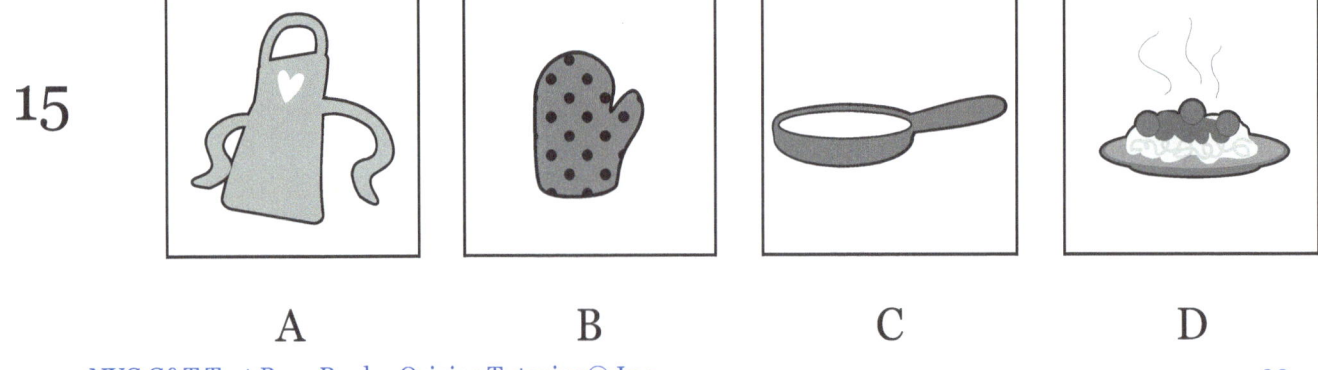

    A   B   C   D

Aural Reasoning

It is Peter's first day of school. He wants to take to school a snack, books, a backpack and a water bottle. When he got to school, he realized he had forgotten his water bottle. Which picture shows what Peter took to school?

16

A   B   C   D

Jonathan and Blair went to the zoo. Jonathan saw three giraffes. Blair saw the giraffes, but he also saw a reptile. Which picture shows what Blair saw?

17

A   B   C   D

Jerry is late for his appointment at the doctor. He wants to get to the doctor's office quickly. Which picture shows what he uses to get to the doctor's office?

18

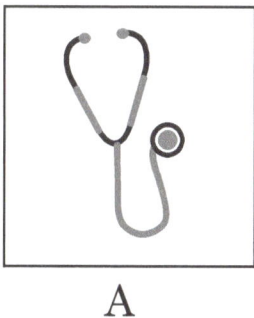  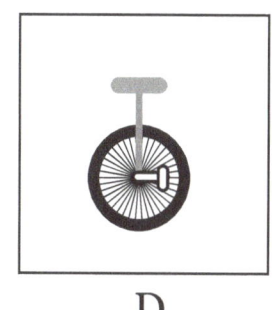

A   B   C   D

Aural Reasoning

Rachel was outside and it started to rain. She went inside to get something to keep her dry. Which picture shows what she chose?

19

A   B   C   D

Three children are waiting in line for buying candies. Bob is standing at the front of the line, Maria is standing behind him and Charlie is standing at the end of the line. Bob is shorter than Maria but taller than Charlie. Which picture shows this?

20

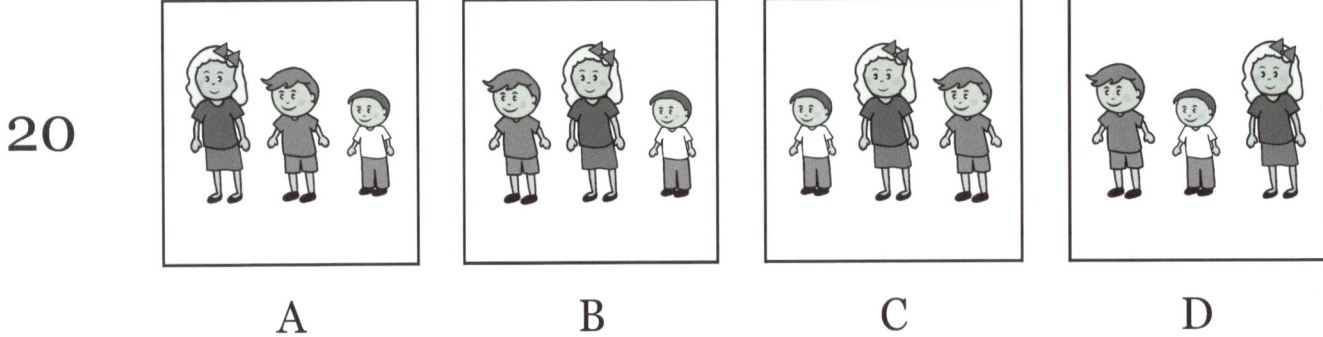

A   B   C   D

Arithmetic Reasoning

The main skill tested by **'Arithmetic Reasoning'** questions is the ability to create mathematical problems from language and to solve those problems.

- These questions test a student's ability to listen to verbal directions that require him or her to count objects, contrast quantities, and solve problems that involve addition, subtraction, multiplication and fractions with small numbers.

- Some of these questions assess basic mathematical concepts, while others assess more so-phisticated concepts such as reasoning and solving word problems.

In this section, you will find **25 "Arithmetic Reasoning"** practice questions to help your student learn the concepts and practice the skills necessary to perform successfully on the official OLSAT® exam.

Tips and Strategies

- Before trying the practice questions in this section, **try using hands-on materials** (like blocks, beads or marbles) to help a student become confident with adding and subtracting. For example, you might give your student two marbles and then ask her to "add" three more marbles to the pile. Then, ask her to count how many marbles she now has. This works with subtraction, too.

- Tell your student to **look at the answer options** while you ask the questions. Ask your student to **eliminate obviously wrong answers** to narrow down the answer choices.

- Ask your student to **explain why he chose a specific answer**. This will help you identify where your student is stumbling, and be an opportunity to reinforce his understanding of the concept and/or calculation.

Arithmetic Reasoning

Lionel went to the library and took out one book. Sally took out two books and Owen took out one book. Which picture shows the books they took out the library?

1

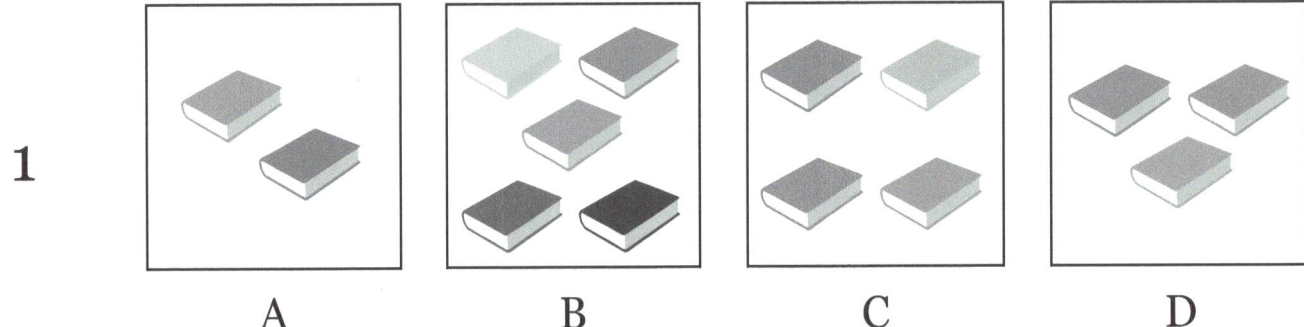

A   B   C   D

Chris takes some rubber ducks into his bath, which you see at the beginning of the row. His mother takes one of the ducks out of the bath. Which picture shows the number of ducks left in the bath?

2

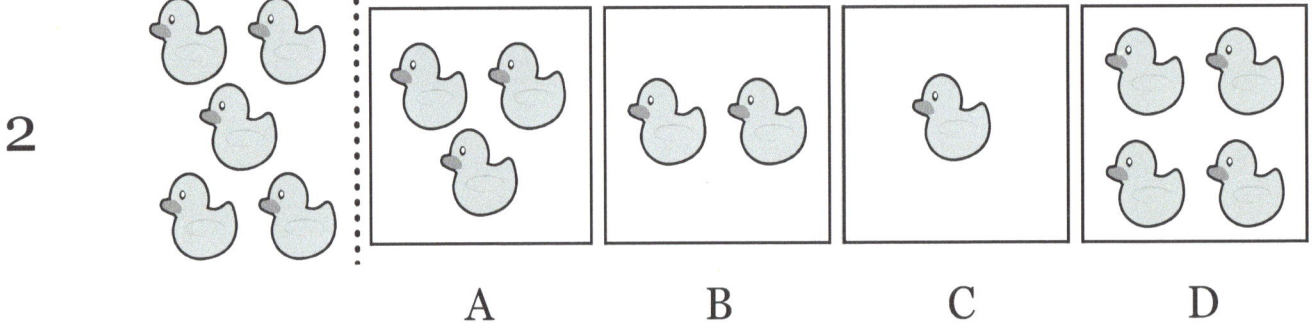

A   B   C   D

The picture at the beginning of the row shows some easter eggs. Lisa and Ben want to share the easter eggs equally. Which picture shows the number of easter eggs Lisa has if the easter eggs are shared equally?

3

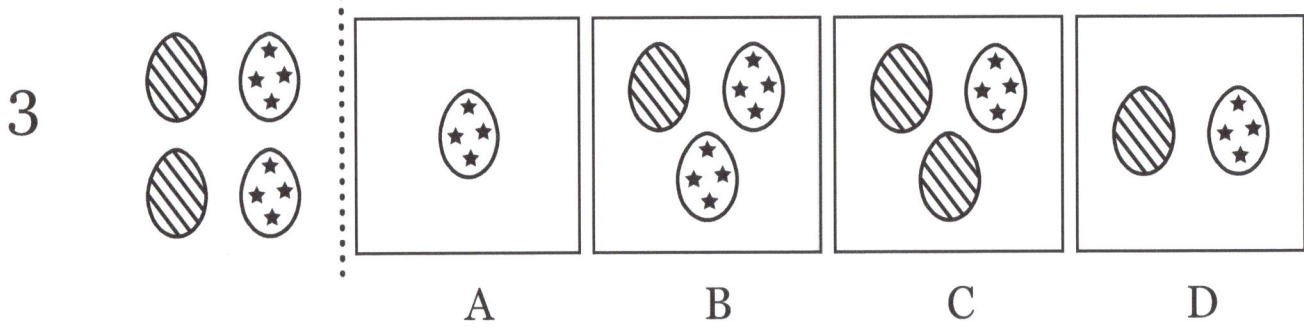

A   B   C   D

Arithmetic Reasoning

Margaret had some candies, which you see at the beginning of the row. Margaret gave three candies to her friend, Sharon. Which picture shows the number of candies Margaret was left with?

4

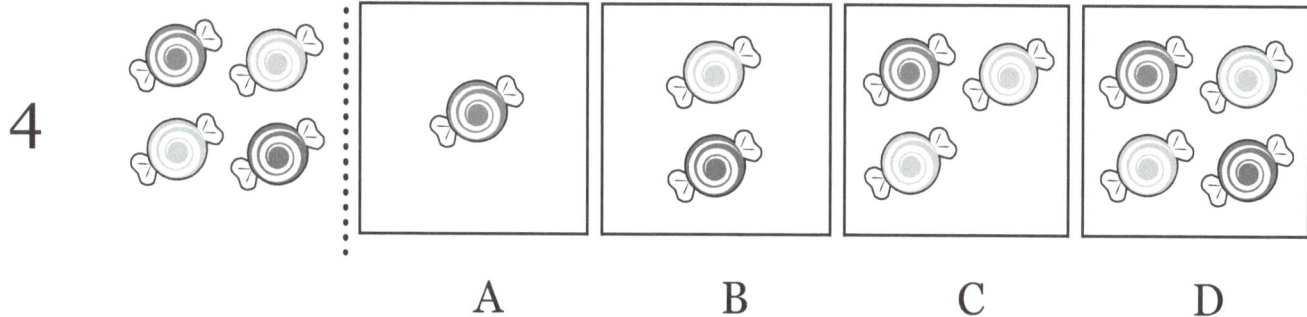

A   B   C   D

Martha has 2 small cups. Felix has 4 larger cups, which you see at the beginning of the row. Felix broke one of his cups and Martha broke one of her cups. Which picture shows the total number of cups that are not broken?

5

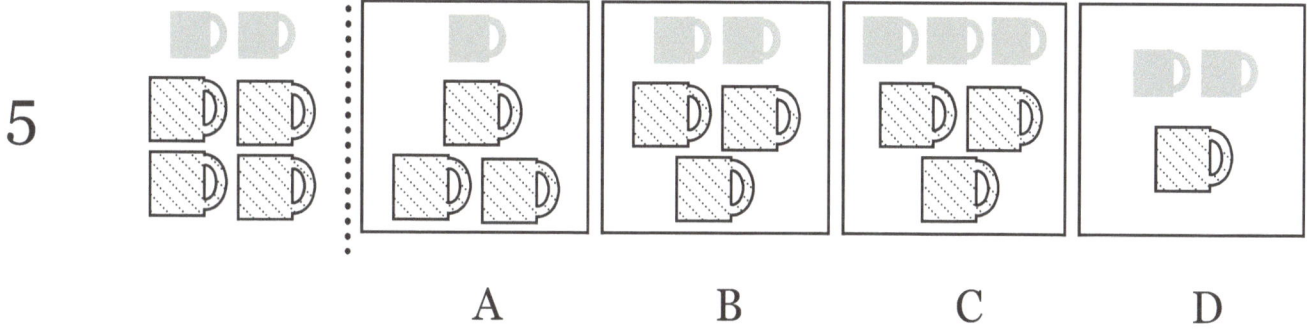

A   B   C   D

Magnus and Katie went fishing and caught six fish, which you see at the beginning of the row. Katie caught two less fish than Magnus. Which picture shows the number of fish that Katie caught?

6

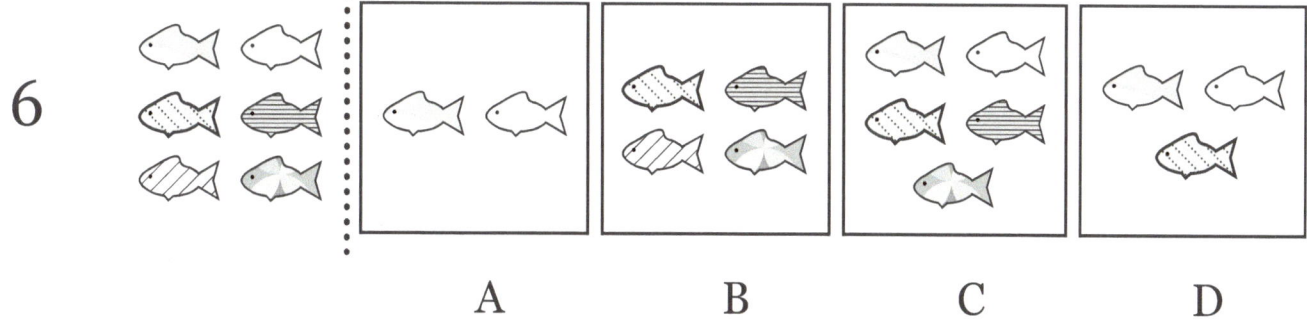

A   B   C   D

Arithmetic Reasoning

In the pet store, Barbara watches a mouse eats two pieces of cheese. She also watches a rabbit eat more pieces of cheese than the mouse, as well as a strawberry. Which picture shows what Barbara saw the rabbit eat?

7

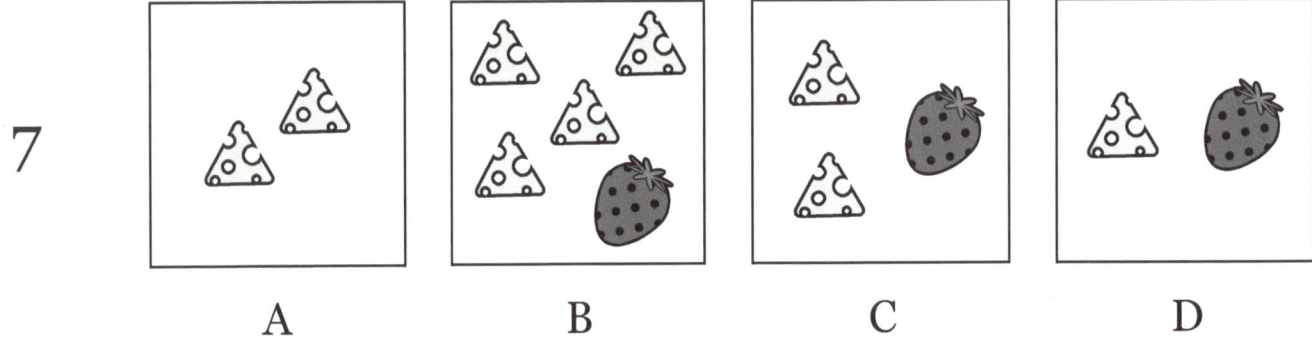

A B C D

In the picture at the beginning of the row is a birthday cake. Florence, Maria, and Michael each took one slice of birthday cake. Which picture shows what the cake looks like after the three children took their slices?

8

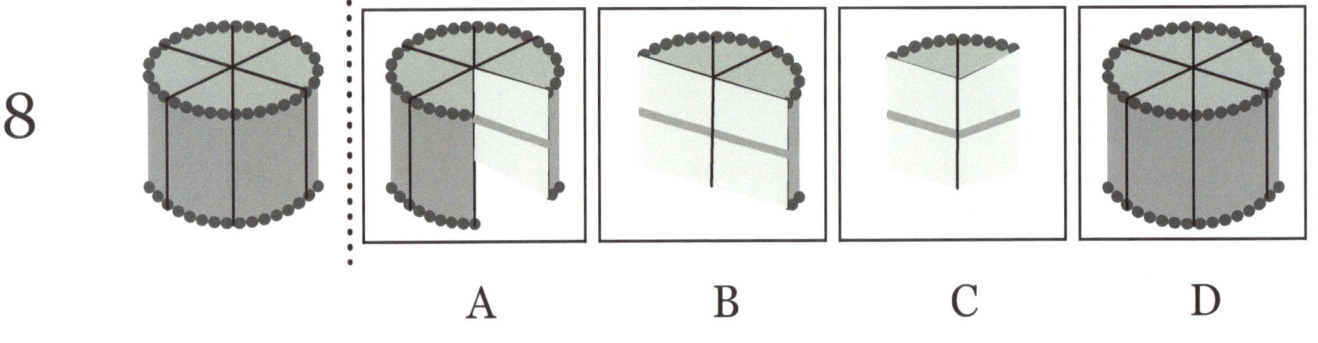

A B C D

The picture at the beginning of the row shows some snowmen that Chris made. Later on, Chris made three more snowmen. Which picture shows the number of snowmen that Chris built altogether?

9

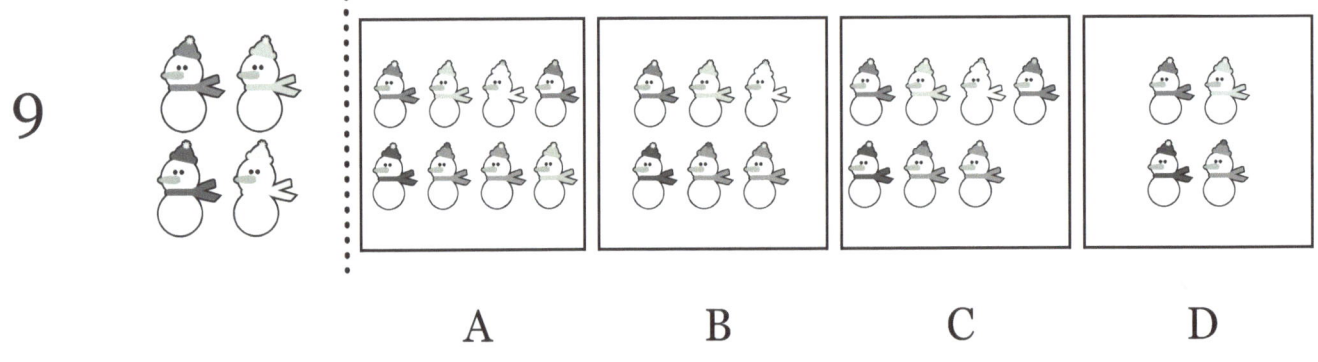

A B C D

Arithmetic Reasoning

At the beginning of the row, you can see some jars and some caps. Which picture shows how many more caps are needed so each jar has a cap?

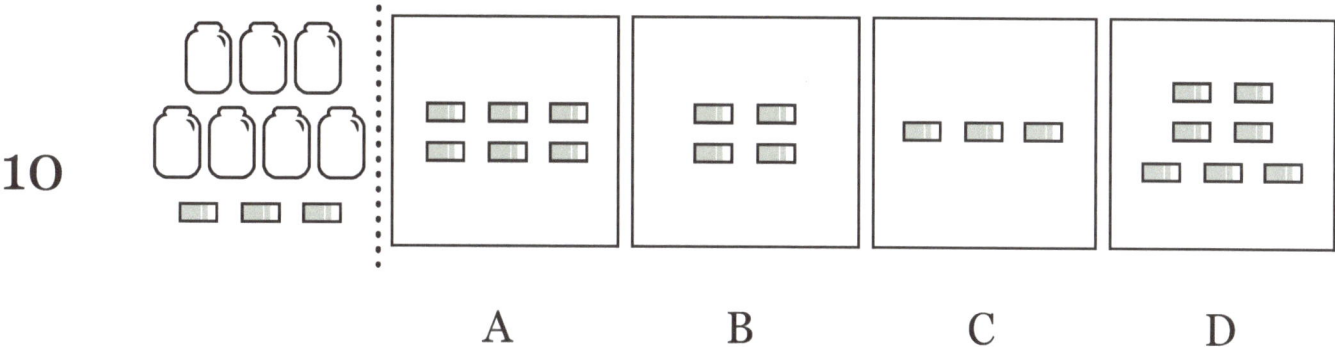

A   B   C   D

Beatrix has some pets, which you see at the beginning of the row. Samuel has three more pets than Beatrix. Which picture shows the number of pets belonging to Samuel?

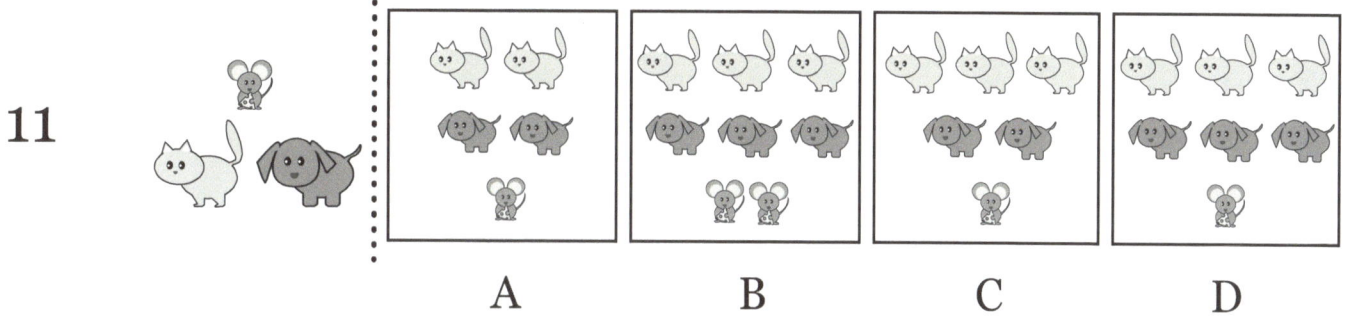

A   B   C   D

The picture at the beginning of the row shows some keys and some locks. Each lock needs its own key. Which picture shows how many more keys are needed so each lock has its own key?

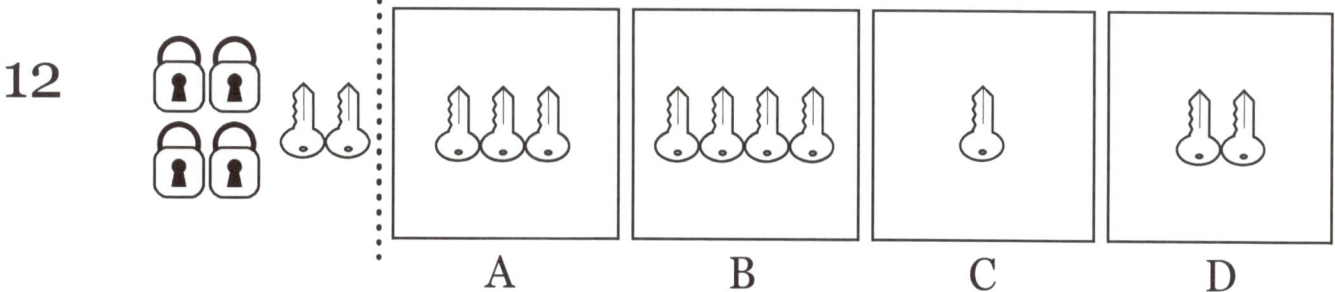

A   B   C   D

Arithmetic Reasoning

13. The picture at the beginning of the row shows a mother. She has four daughters and two sons. Which picture shows the children of this mother?

A   B   C   D

14. John and Daniel want to get some crayons from the drawer. They want three crayons each. Which picture shows the total number of crayons they need to get?

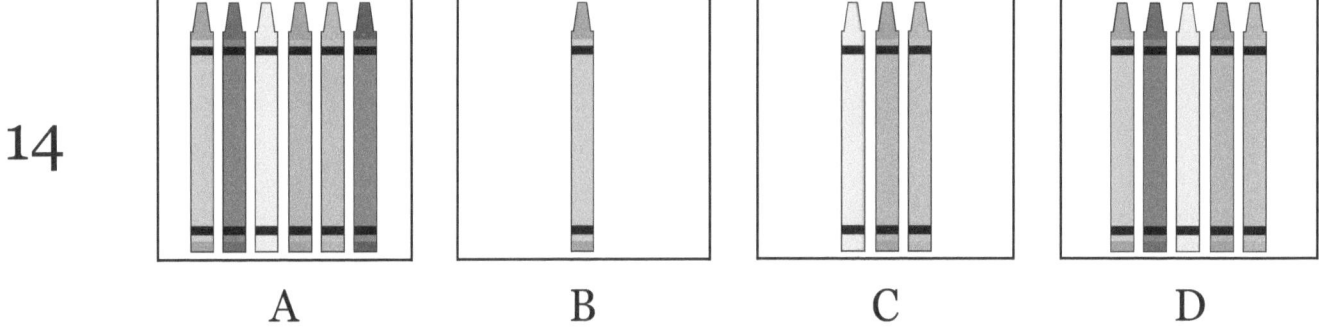

A   B   C   D

15. The picture at the beginning of the row shows a pizza. Charles and Karyn ate two slices of pizza each. Which picture shows what the pizza looks like after the two children ate their slices?

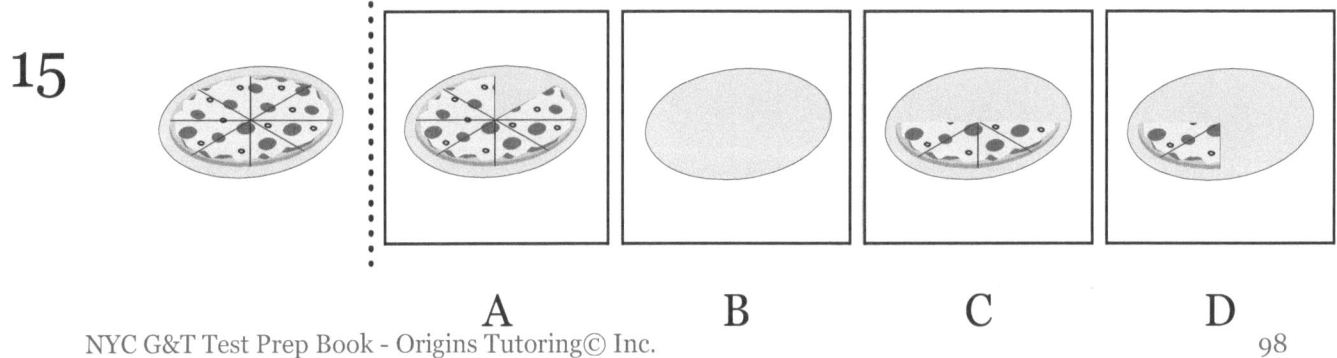

A   B   C   D

Arithmetic Reasoning

The zookeeper needs to feed three monkeys and four lions. At the beginning of the row, you can see how many lions and monkeys the zookeeper has fed. Which picture shows how many more monkeys and lions he needs to feed?

Peter ate some hotdogs and a hamburger at the carnival, which you see at the beginning of the row. Liam ate one more hotdog and two more hamburgers than Peter. Which picture shows what Liam ate at the carnival?

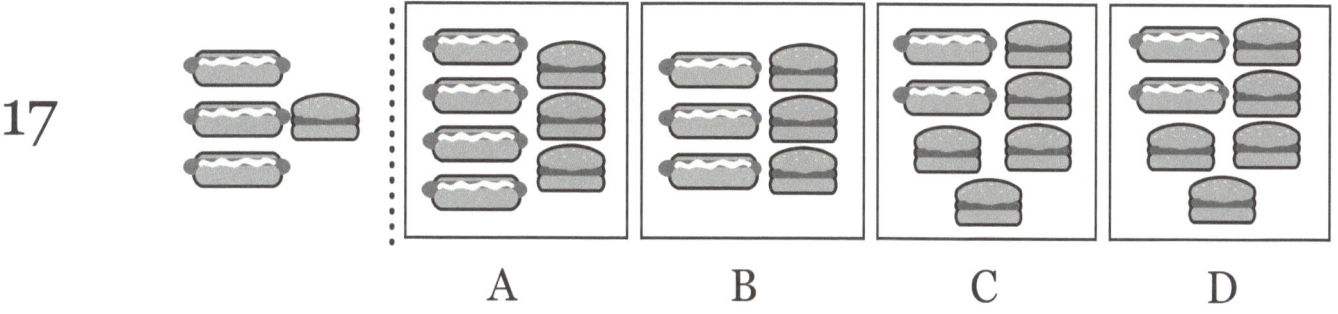

Kylie has some hats, which you can see at the beginning of the row. Kylie gives six of the hats to her mother. Which picture shows how many hats Kylie has left?

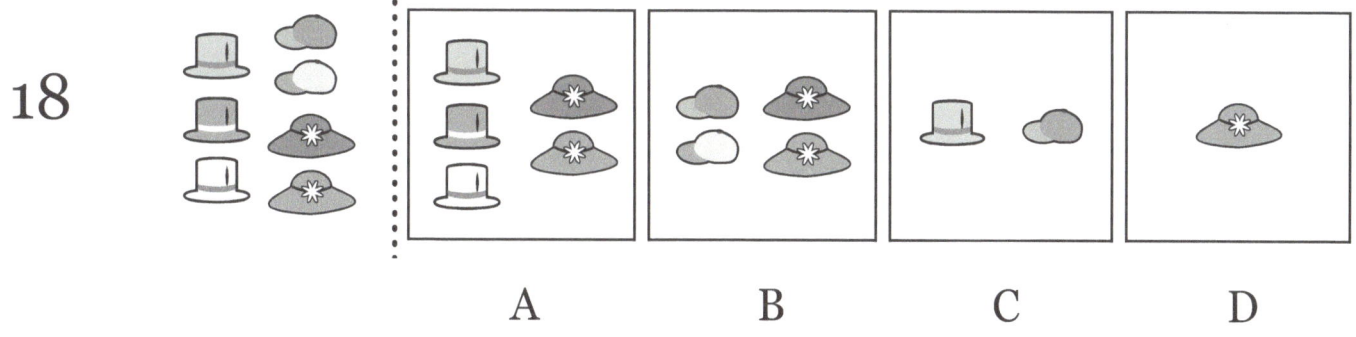

Arithmetic Reasoning

A farmer owns some buckets, which you see at the beginning of the row. The farmer wants to buy five more buckets. Which picture shows the total number of buckets the farmer wants to own?

19

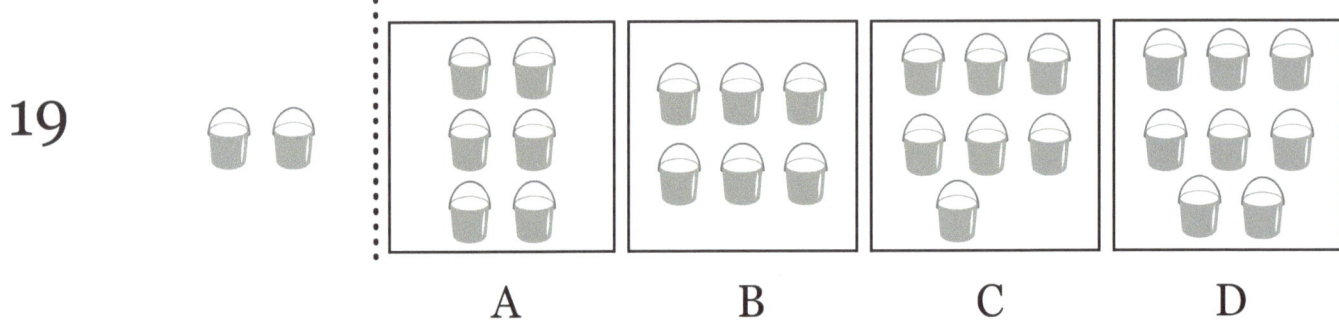

Melania has some cups and plates, which you see at the beginning of the row. Patricia has fewer plates than Melania but more cups. Which picture shows the cups and plates Patricia has?

20

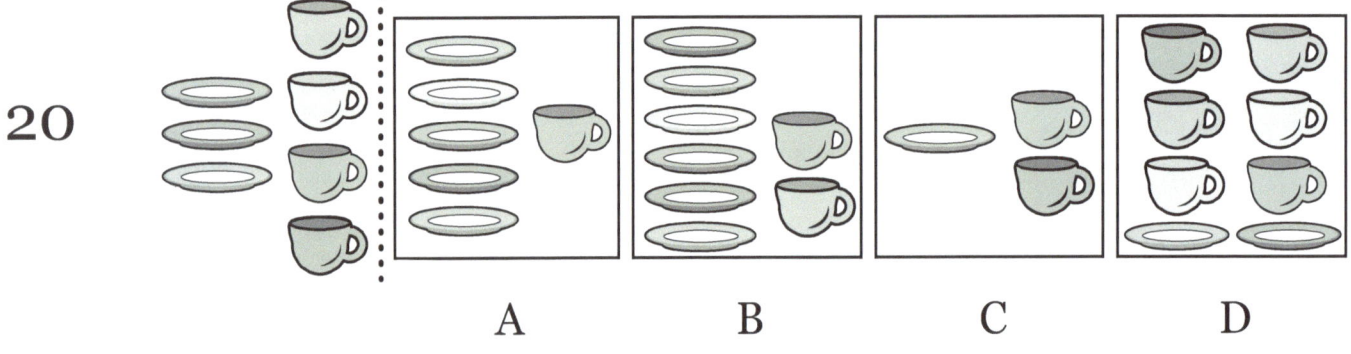

The picture at the beginning of the row shows some balloons that Ralph blew up. Sally blew up three more balloons than Ralph. Which picture shows the number of balloons Sally blew up?

21

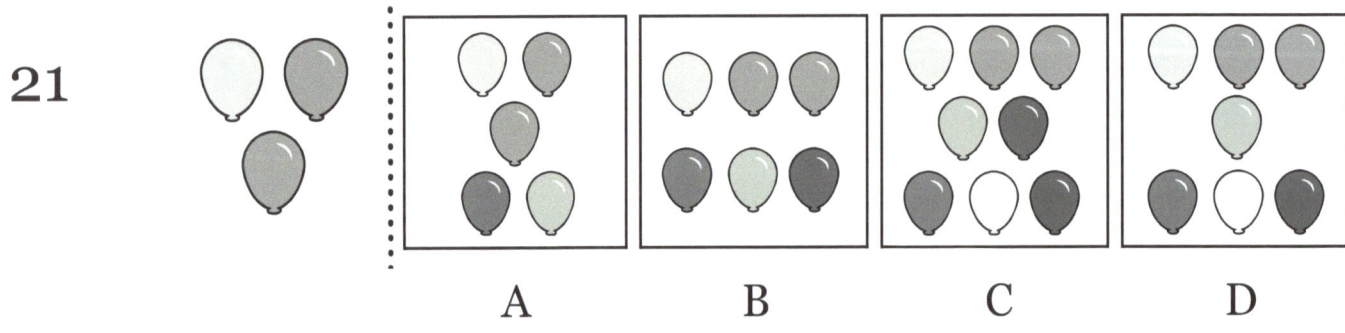

Arithmetic Reasoning

In a pond are some frogs and some lilypads, which you see at the beginning of the row. Some frogs have a lilypad and the others don't have a lilypad. How many more lilypads are needed so that each frog can have a lilypad? Which picture shows this?

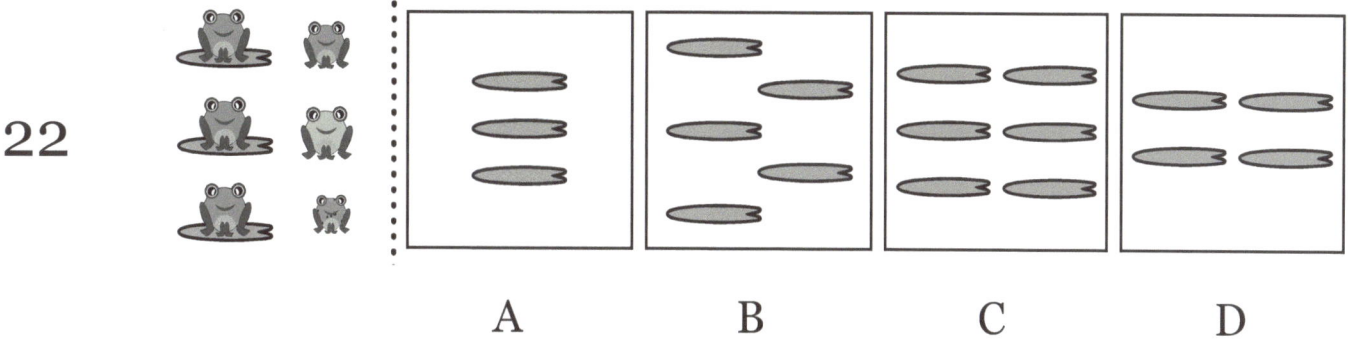

          A   B   C   D

Karyn went to the zoo and saw one black snake, two striped snakes, and two gray snakes. Which picture shows what Karyn saw at the zoo?

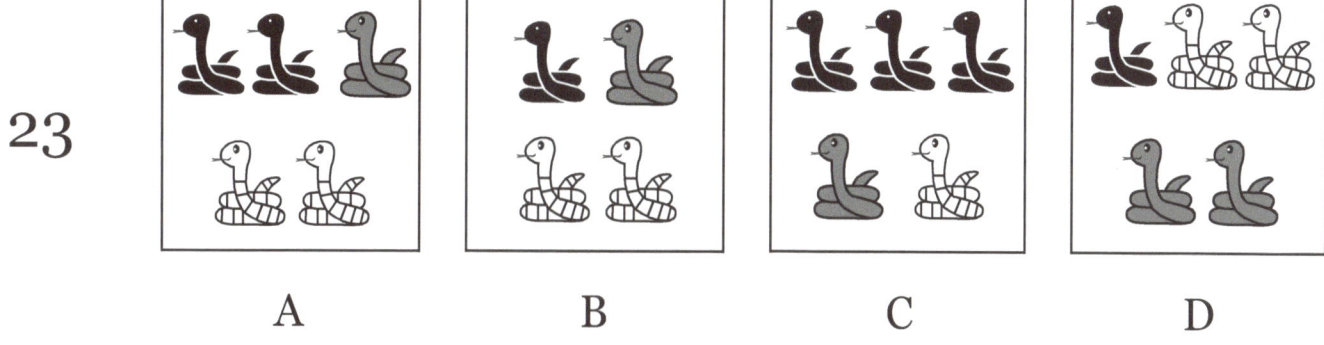

          A   B   C   D

William has some seashells, which you can see at the beginning of the row. William gave two seashells to Victor and gave one to Ross. Which picture shows how many seashells William has left?

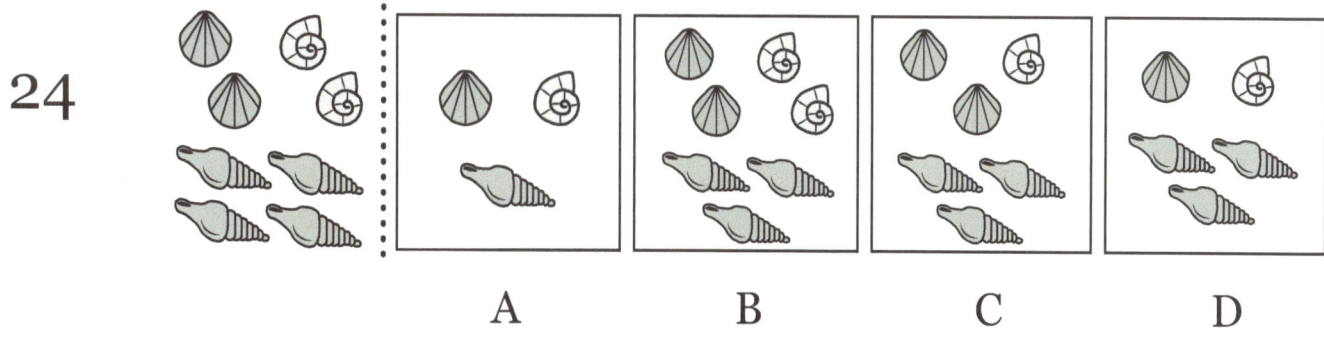

          A   B   C   D

Arithmetic Reasoning

Farrah, Alice and Benjamin shared a birthday cake, which you can see at the beginning of the row. Farrah ate one slice, Benjamin ate two slices and Alice ate one slice. Which picture shows what the leftover birthday cake looked like?

25

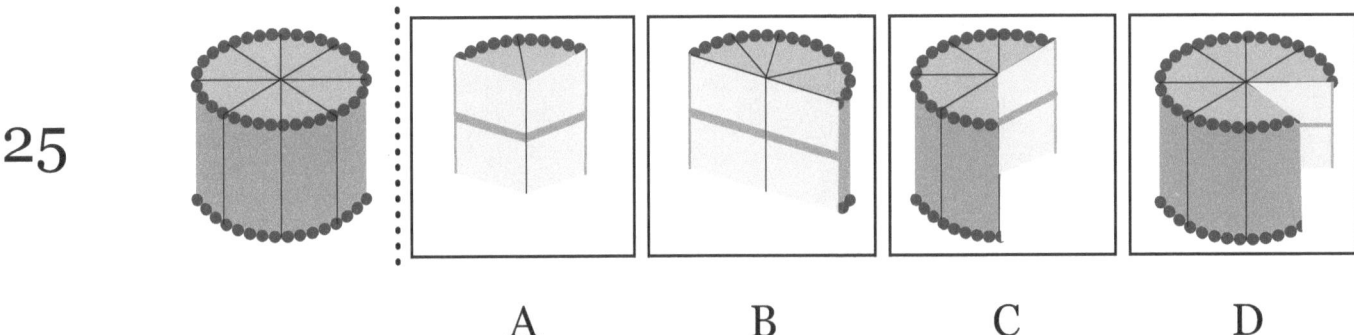

A   B   C   D

OLSAT® Level A Test Prep Answers

Following Directions	
1	D
2	A
3	B
4	C
5	B
6	A
7	C
8	A
9	D
10	B
11	B
12	C
13	A
14	B
15	B
16	D
17	C
18	C
19	D
20	C
21	D
22	C
23	B
24	A
25	B

Aural Reasoning	
1	C
2	B
3	B
4	A
5	D
6	D
7	A
8	C
9	C
10	A
11	C
12	B
13	A
14	C
15	B
16	C
17	A
18	C
19	D
20	B

Arithmetic Reasoning	
1	C
2	D
3	D
4	A
5	A
6	A
7	B
8	B
9	C
10	B
11	C
12	D
13	D
14	A
15	C
16	B
17	A
18	D
19	C
20	D
21	B
22	A
23	D
24	D
25	B

OLSAT® A
Supplemental Games and Activities

This book provides practice questions to help students get used to official OLSAT® questions. In addition to doing practice questions, there are many other supplemental activities that can help a student strengthen his or her short-term memory and improve listening and logical reasoning skills measured by the OLSAT®.

These include:

- Enhancing background knowledge and expanding visual vocabulary by visiting places such as a zoo, museum, circus, farm or aquarium, where a child can encounter objects and animals in context.

- Playing traditional memory games such as 'Matching Pairs', the 'Ever-increasing Shopping List' (I went to the shop and bought a....), and 'Which Item is Missing?', where items are placed and named on the table, then one object is removed.

- Using picture flashcards to help your child classify how different items share a common category because of shared characteristics.

- Engaging in play experiences that involve naming and sorting and classifying common objects, including types of clothing, furniture, tools, vehicles, animals, vegetables, fruits and plants. For example:

  - One player (without telling the others) chooses a common object (eg: an orange) and uses specific words to describe which category it belongs to, and other defining concepts such as its color, shape, size, use, location, etc. ("I'm thinking of a fruit that is round, orange, juicy, grows on trees, makes juice). The other player/s guess what is being described.
  - Players choose a word category (e.g., footwear) and try to describe as many objects as possible that are part of the category (include sneakers, shoes, boots, sandals, socks, slippers).
  - Players choose a topic (eg: cats) and together try to think of familiar concepts related to it (include has four legs, has whiskers, runs away from dogs, can be a pet, purrs).

www.ingramcontent.com/pod-product-compliance
Lightning Source LLC
Chambersburg PA
CBHW040053160426
43192CB00002B/56